E-Z PLAY TODAY

46

15 CHART HITS

M000106546

ISBN 978-1-4950-5815-8

HAL•LEONARD® CORPORATION

7777 W. BLUEMOUND RD. P.O. BOX 13819 MILWAUKEE, WI 53213

Visit Hal Leonard Online at
www.halleonard.com

CONTENTS

All About That Bass

Registration 2
Rhythm: Pop or Rock

Words and Music by Kevin Kadish
and Meghan Trainor

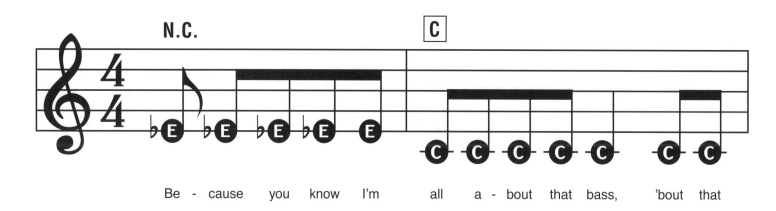

Be - cause you know I'm all a - bout that bass, 'bout that

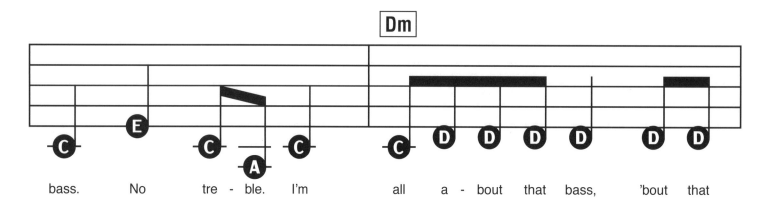

bass. No tre - ble. I'm all a - bout that bass, 'bout that

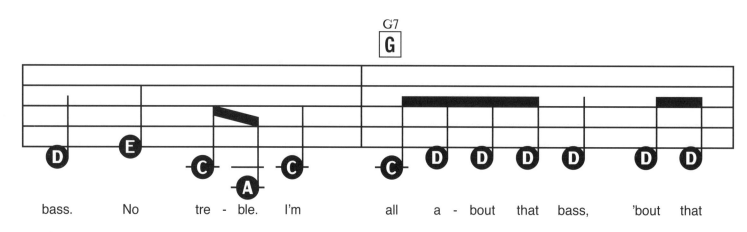

bass. No tre - ble. I'm all a - bout that bass, 'bout that

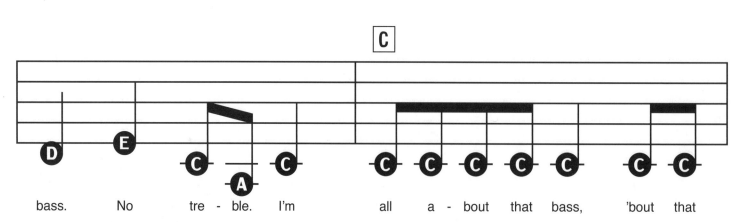

bass. No tre - ble. I'm all a - bout that bass, 'bout that

N.C.

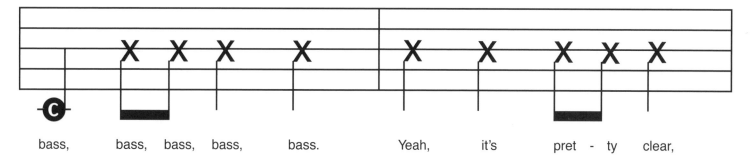

bass,   bass, bass, bass,   bass.   Yeah,   it's   pret - ty   clear,

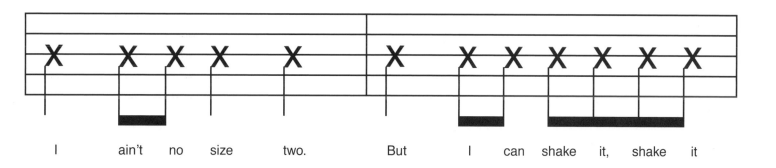

I   ain't no size   two.   But   I   can shake it, shake it

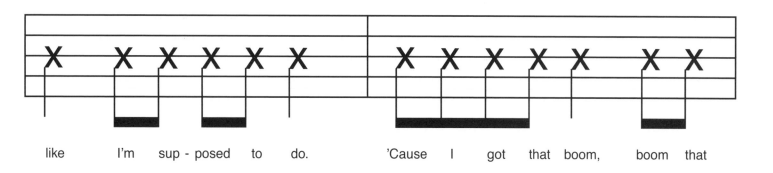

like   I'm sup - posed to do.   'Cause I   got that boom,   boom that

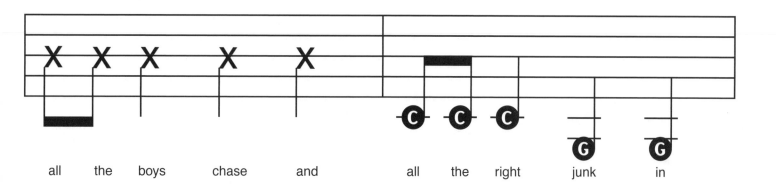

all   the boys   chase   and   all   the right   junk   in

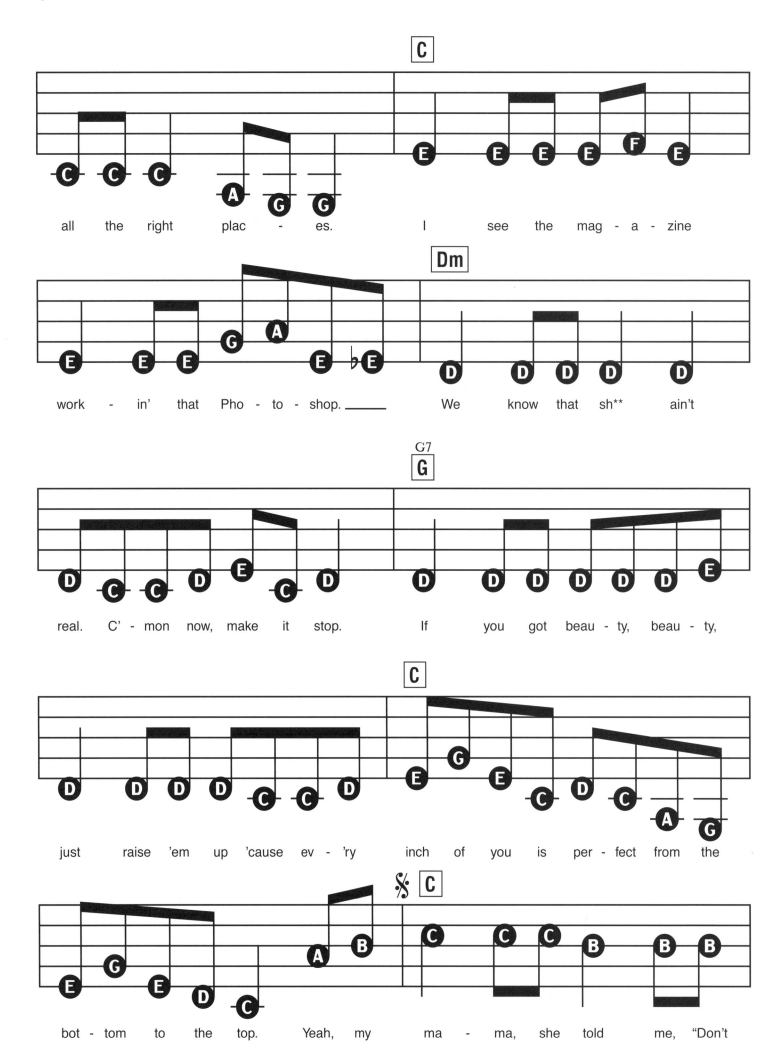

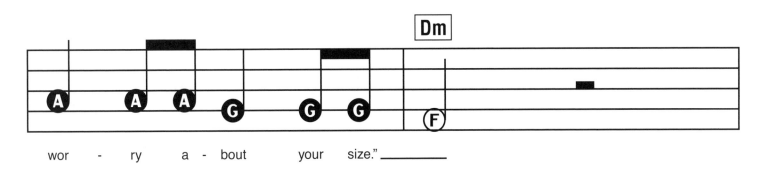

Dm

wor - ry a - bout your size." _____

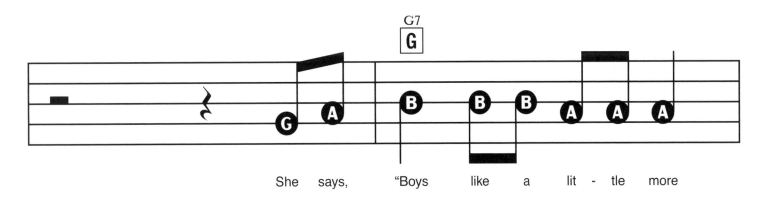

G7
G

She says, "Boys like a lit - tle more

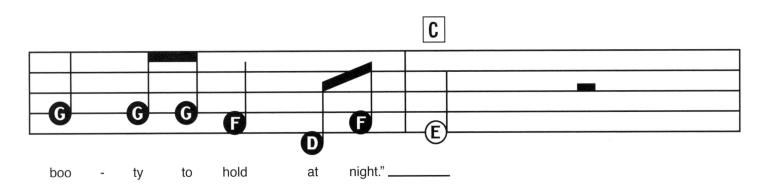

C

boo - ty to hold at night." _____

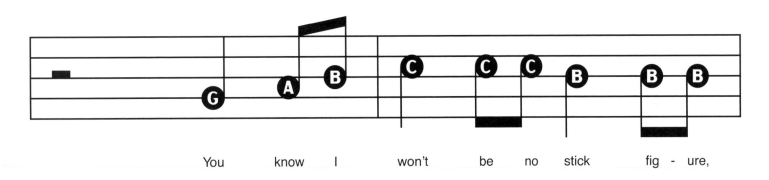

You know I won't be no stick fig - ure,

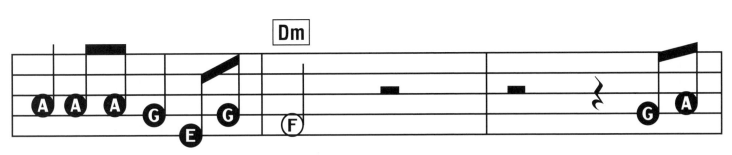

Dm

sil - i - cone Bar - bie doll. _____   So, if

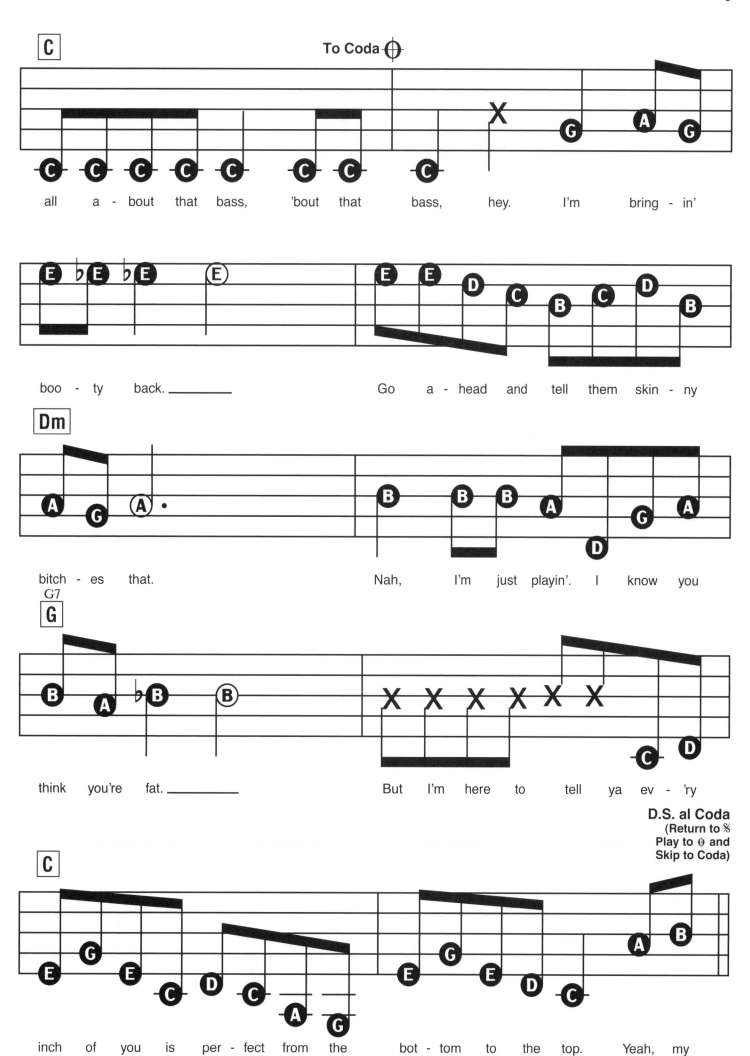

10

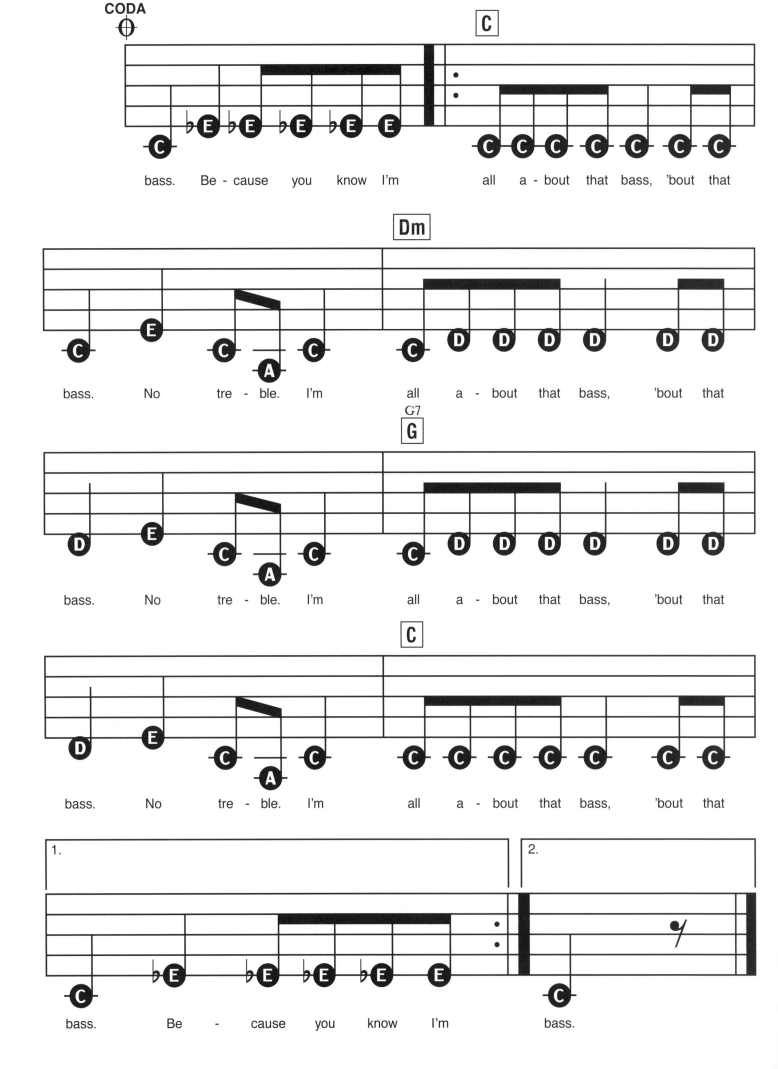

Ex's & Oh's

Registration 2
Rhythm: Shuffle or Rock

Words and Music by Tanner Schneider
and Dave Bassett

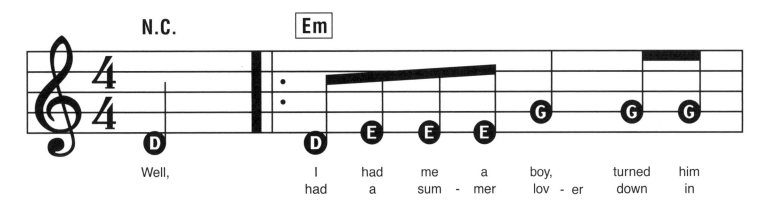

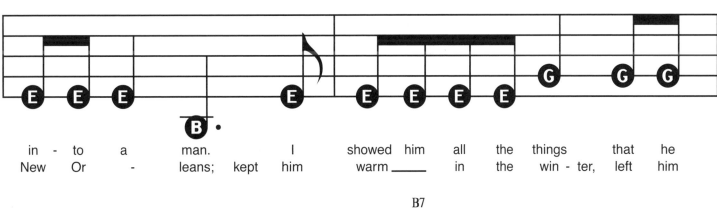

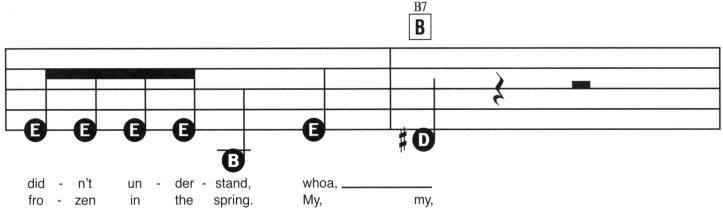

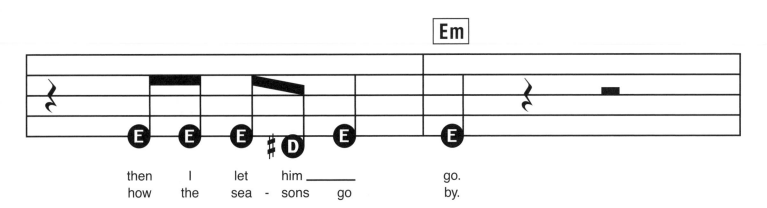

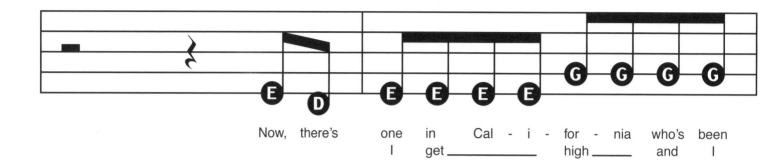

Now, there's one in Cal - i - for - nia who's been
I get _____ high _____ and I

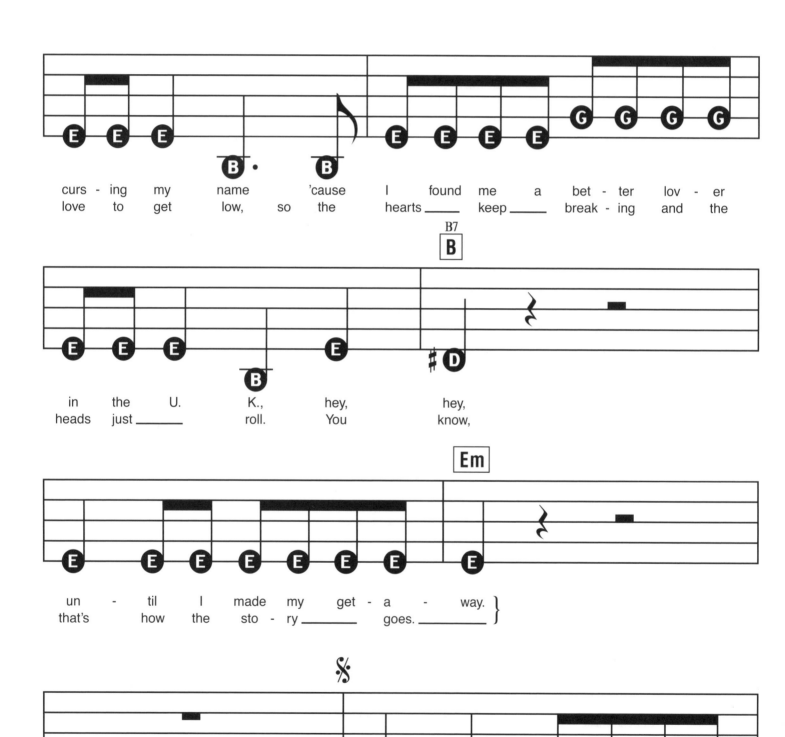

curs - ing my name 'cause I found me a bet - ter lov - er
love to get low, so the hearts _____ me keep _____ break - ing and the

B7

in the U. K., hey, hey,
heads just _____ roll. You know,

Em

un - til I made my get - a - way.
that's how the sto - ry _____ goes. _____

One, two, three, they gon - na

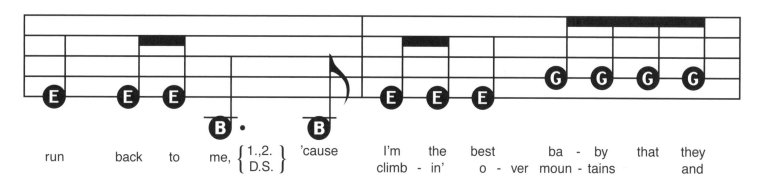

run   back   to   me, { 1.,2. } 'cause   I'm   the   best   ba - by   that   they
                            { D.S. } climb - in'   o - ver   moun - tains   and

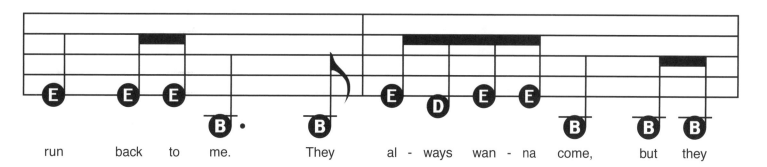

nev - er   got - ta   keep. }
sail - in'   o - ver   seas. }   One,   two,   three,   they   gon - na

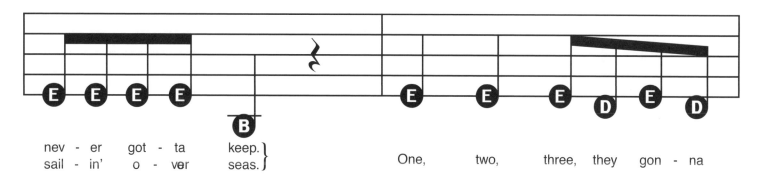

run   back   to   me.   They   al - ways   wan - na   come,   but   they

G

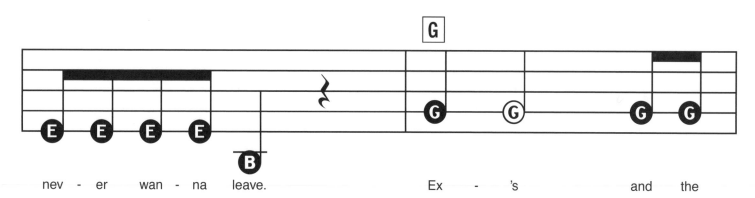

nev - er   wan - na   leave.   Ex - 's   and   the

D   **Em**   **B**

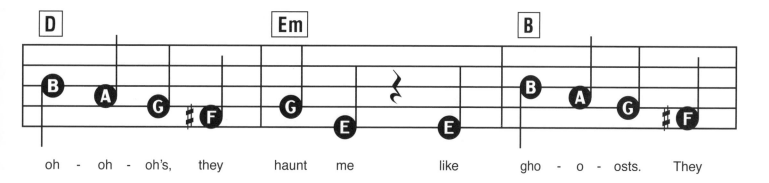

oh - oh - oh's,   they   haunt   me   like   gho - o - osts.   They

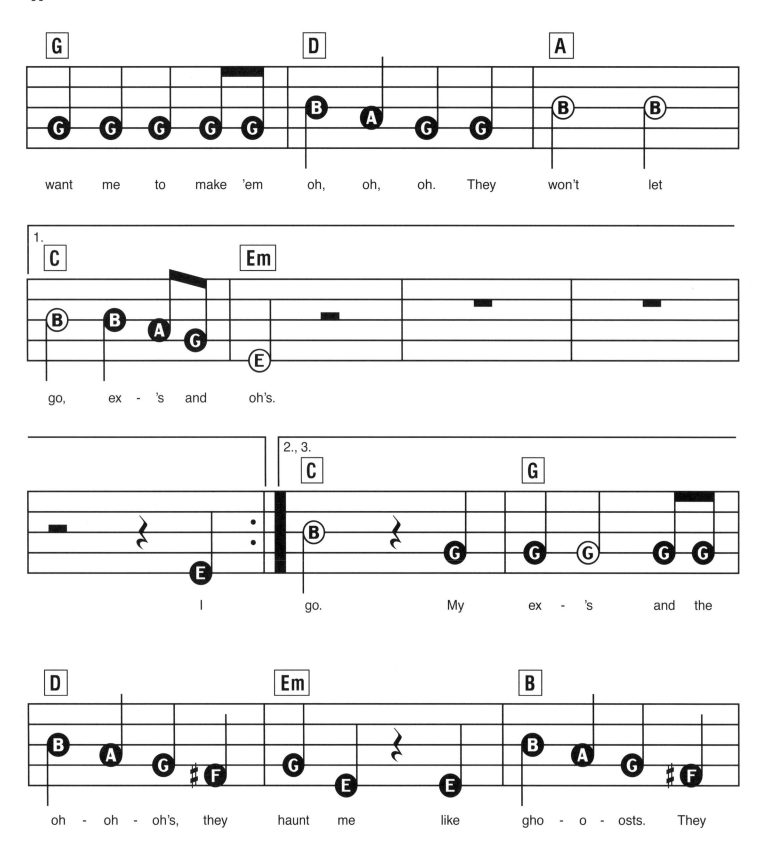

want me to make 'em   oh, oh, oh. They   won't   let

1.
go,   ex - 's and   oh's.

2., 3.
I   go.   My   ex - 's   and   the

oh - oh - oh's,   they   haunt   me   like   gho - o - osts.   They

To Coda

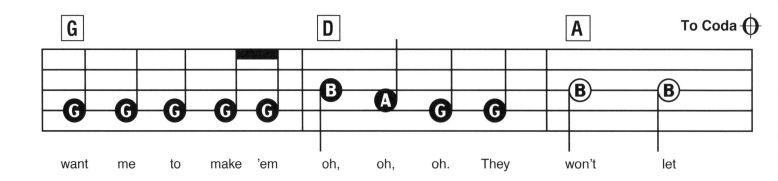

want   me   to   make   'em   oh,   oh,   oh.   They   won't   let

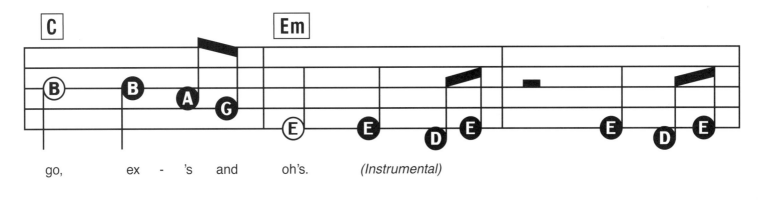

go,   ex - 's   and   oh's.   *(Instrumental)*

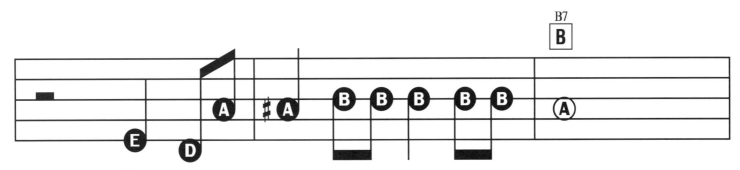

D.S. al Coda
(Return to 𝄋
Play to ⊕ and
Skip to Coda)

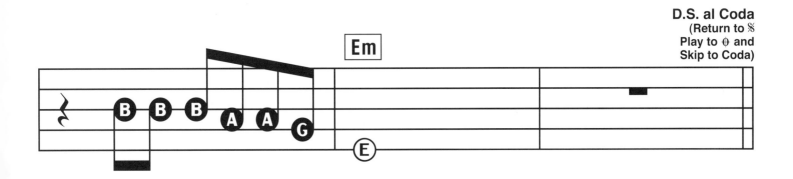

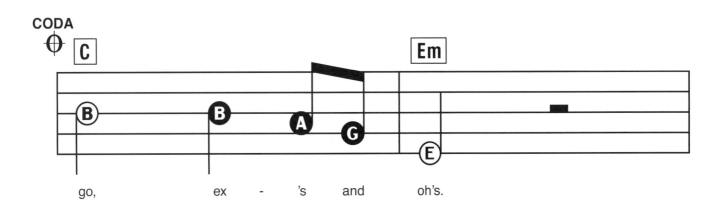

go,   ex - 's   and   oh's.

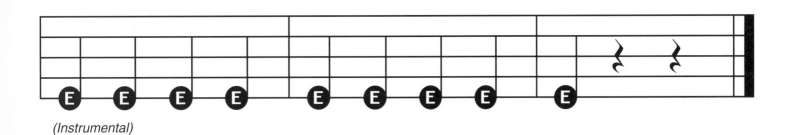

(Instrumental)

Budapest

Registration 4
Rhythm: Country Rock or Rock

Words and Music by George Barnett
and Joel Pott

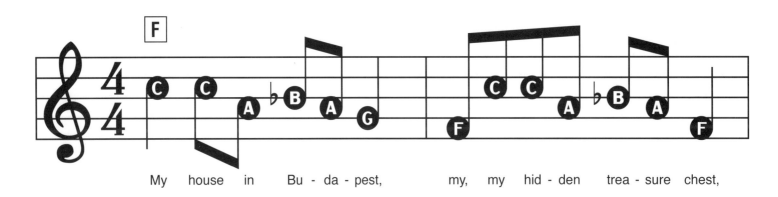

My house in Bu - da - pest, my, my hid - den trea - sure chest,

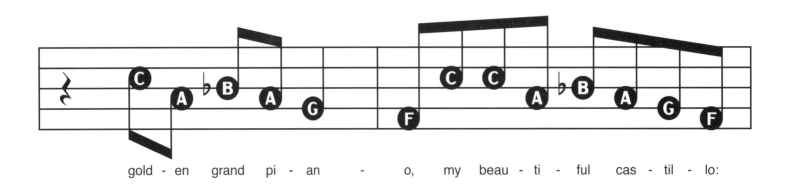

gold - en grand pi - an - o, my beau - ti - ful cas - til - lo:

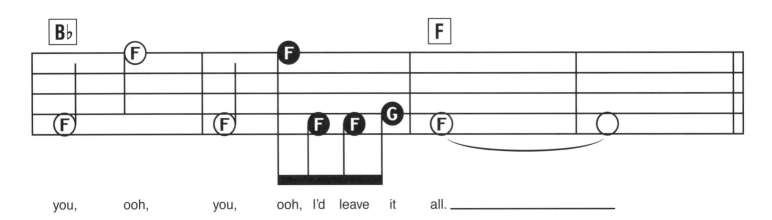

you, ooh, you, ooh, I'd leave it all._____

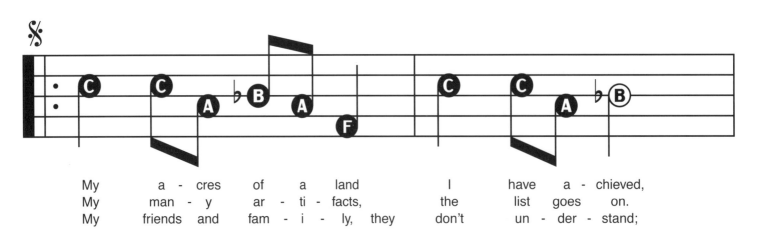

My a - cres of a land I have a - chieved,
My man - y ar - ti - facts, the list goes on.
My friends and fam - i - ly, they don't un - der - stand;

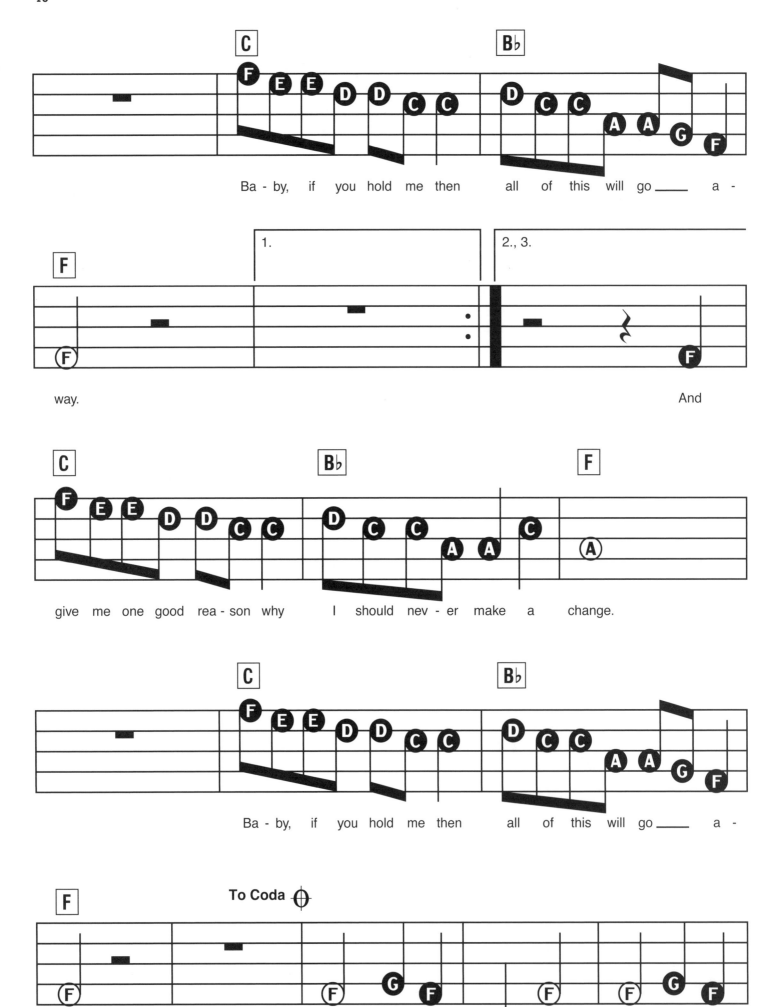

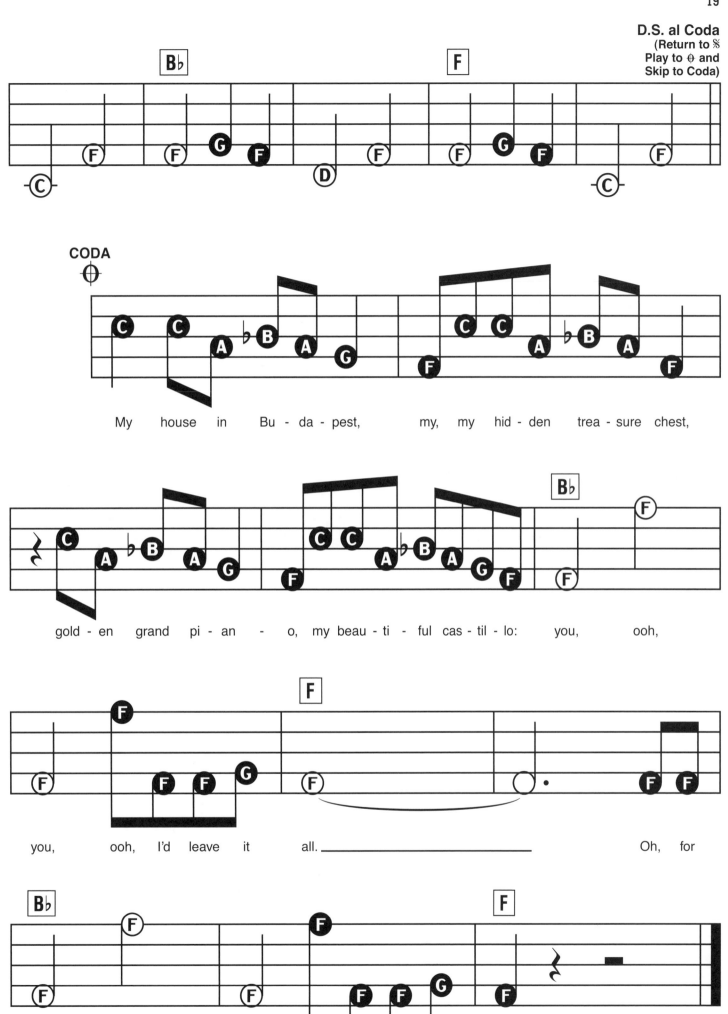

Can't Feel My Face

Registration 2
Rhythm: Funk or Rock

Words and Music by Abel Tesfaye, Max Martin,
Savan Kotecha, Peter Svensson and Ali Payami

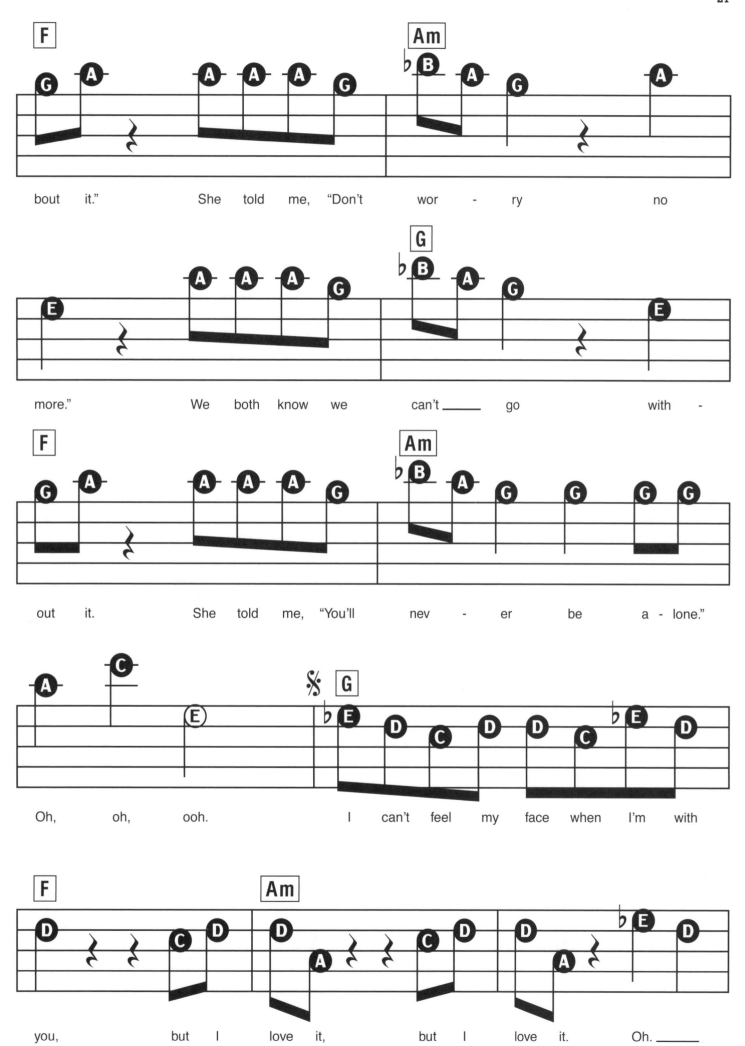

22

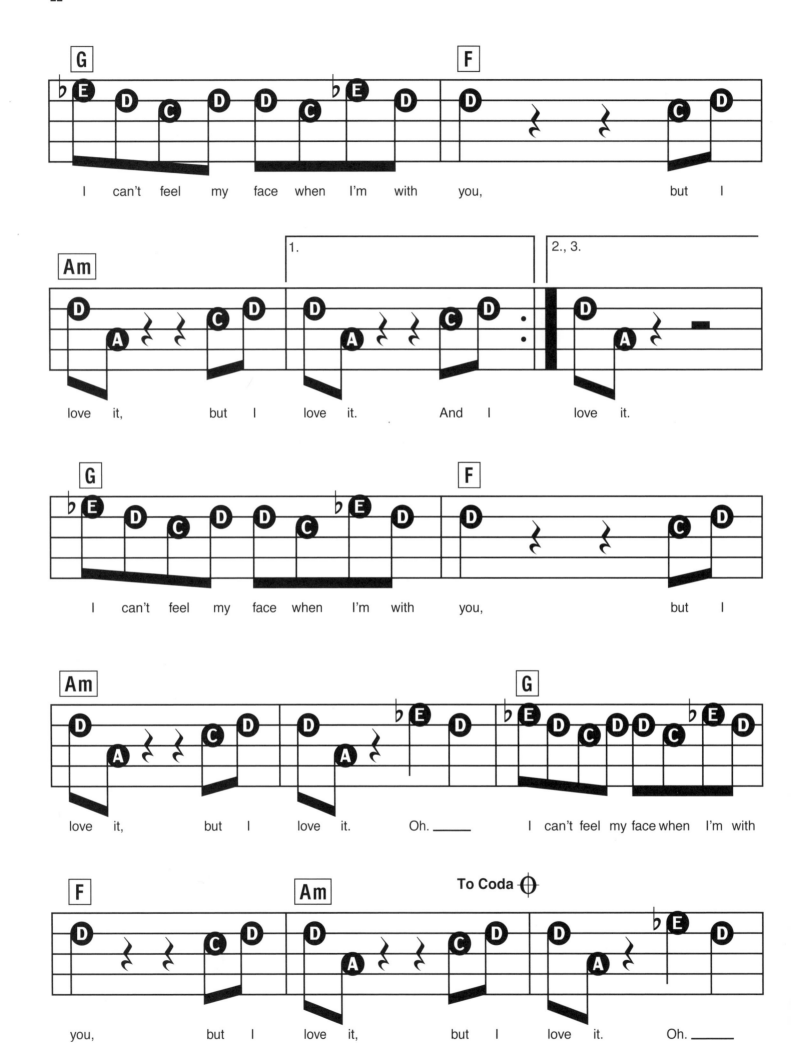

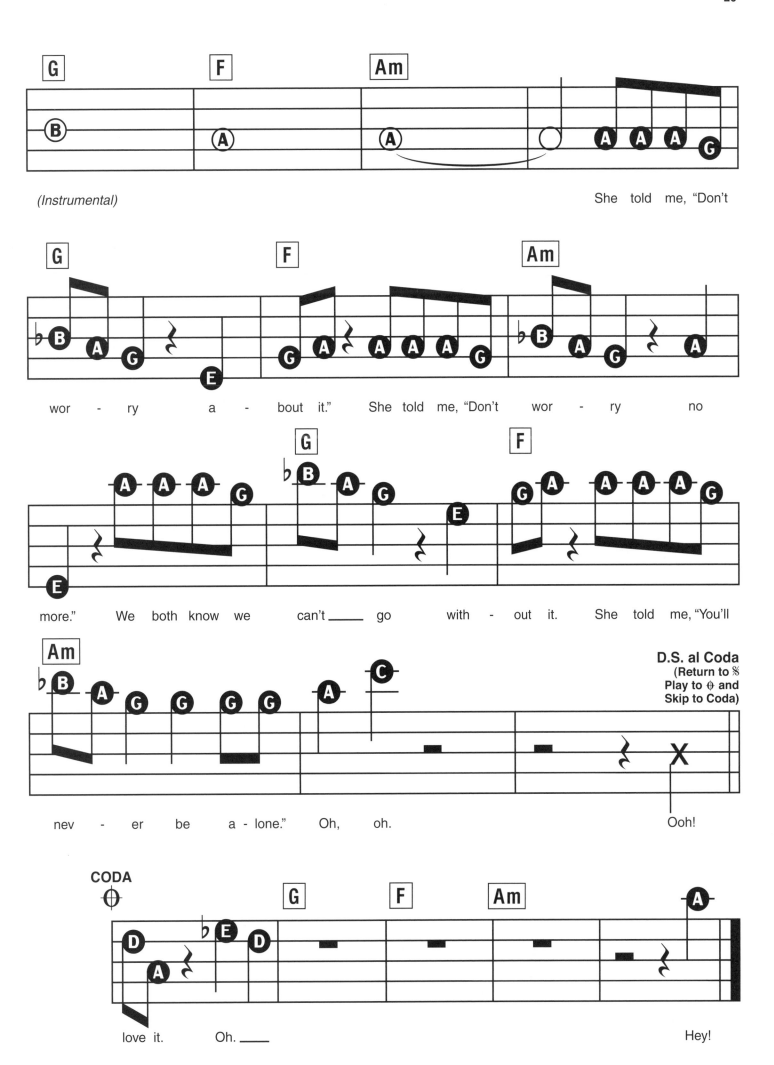

Drag Me Down

Registration 4
Rhythm: Pop Rock or Rock

Words and Music by John Henry Ryan,
Jamie Scott and Julian Bunetta

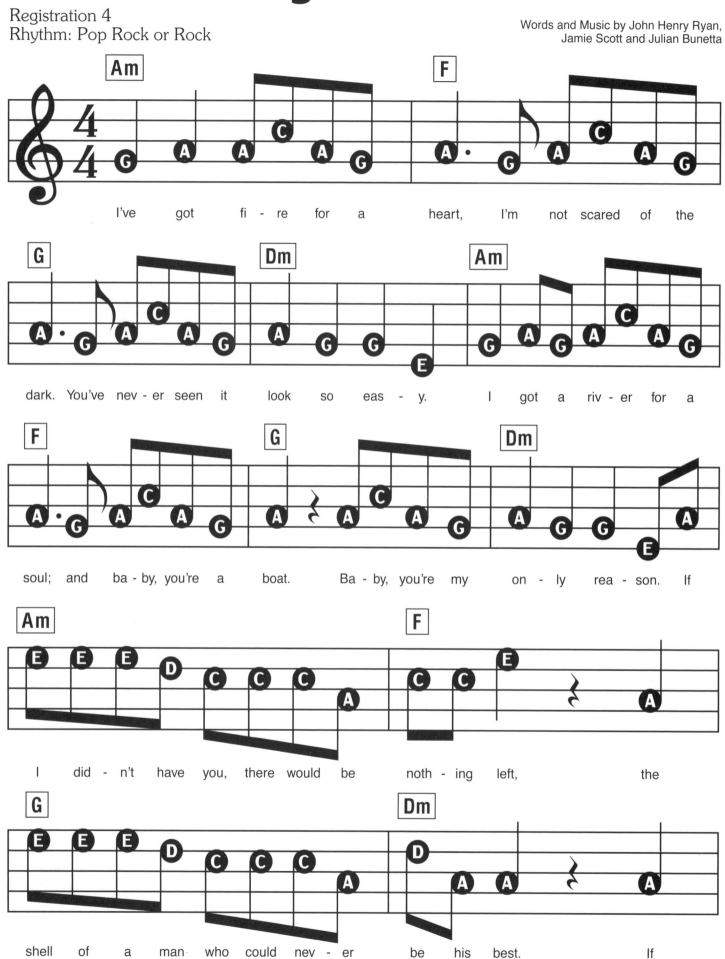

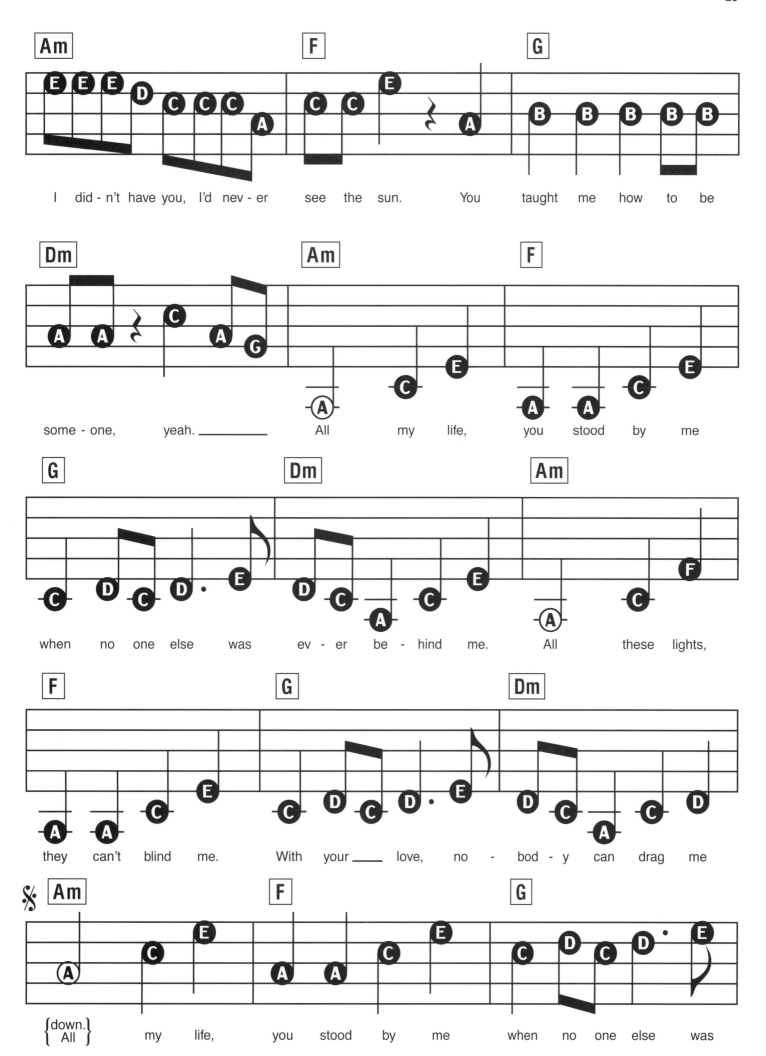

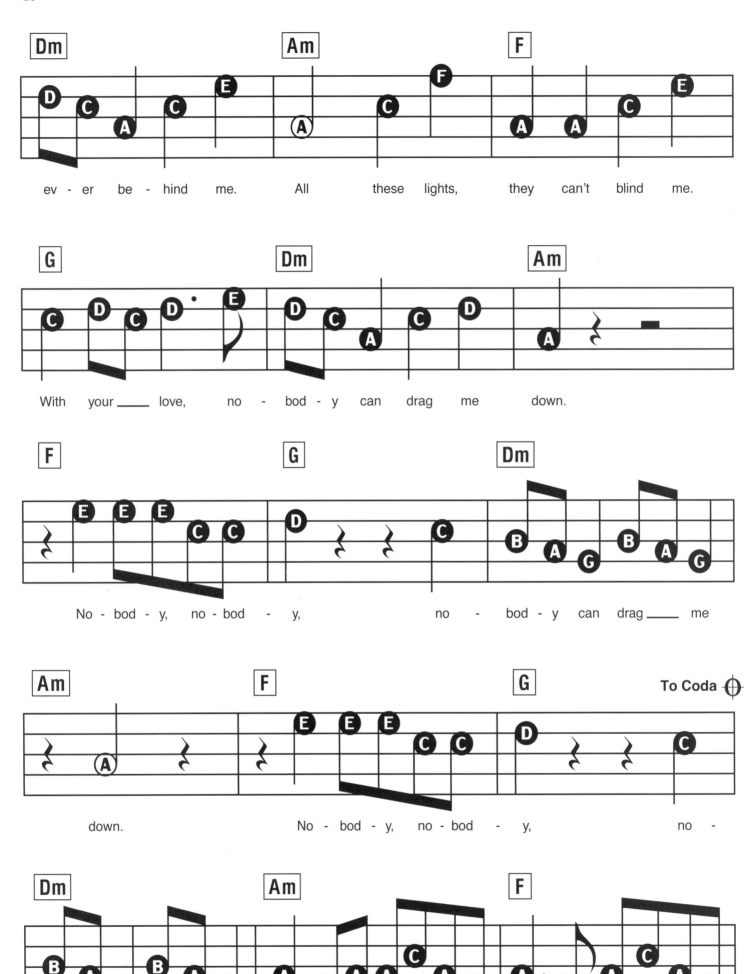

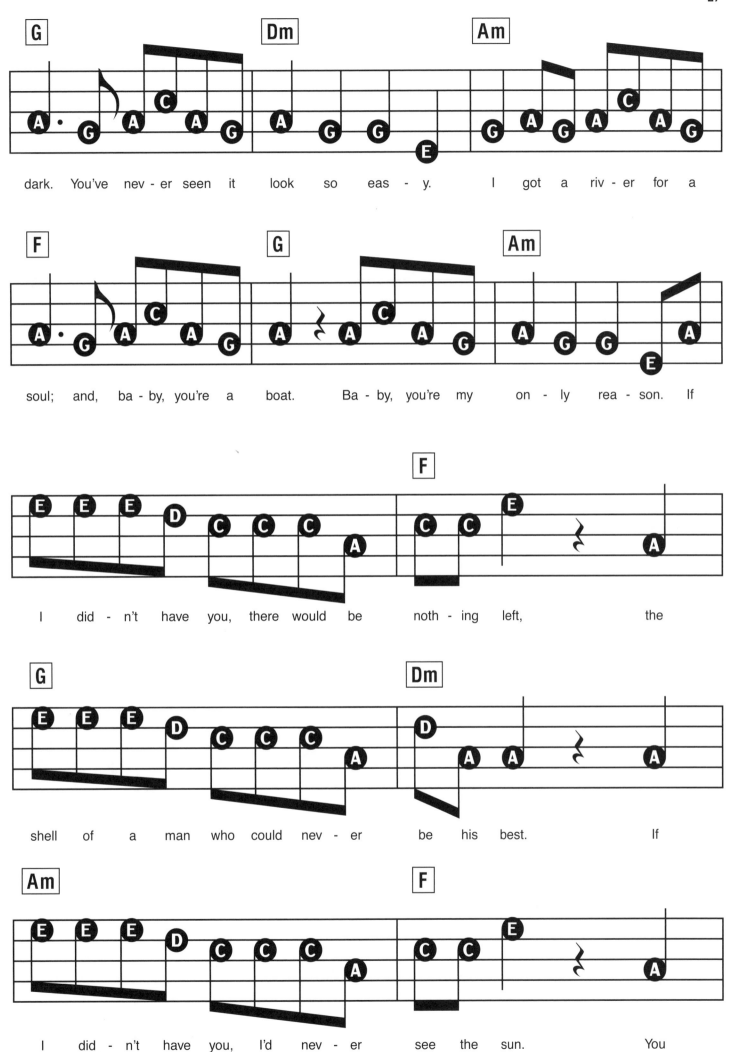

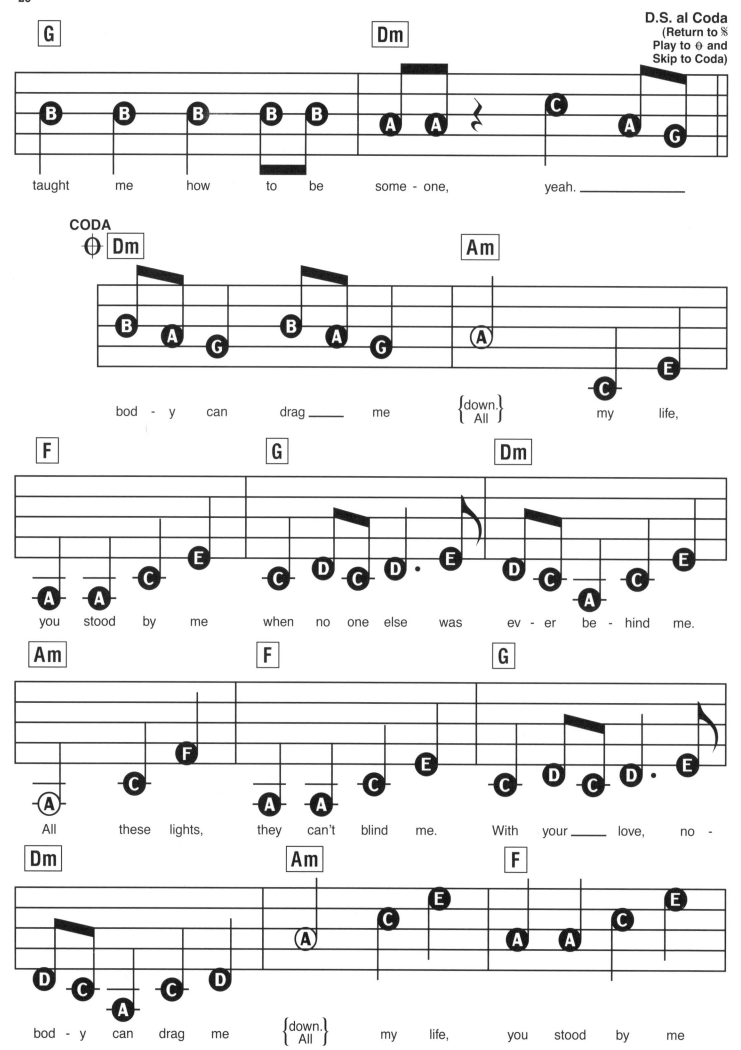

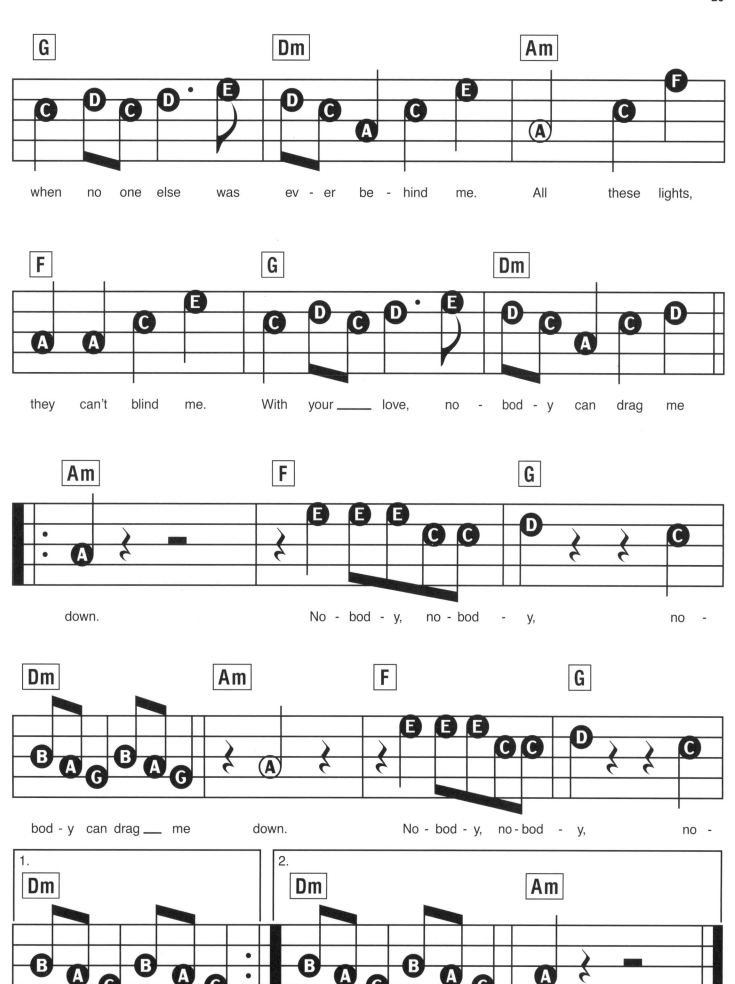

Hello

Registration 8
Rhythm: Ballad

Words and Music by Adele Adkins
and Greg Kurstin

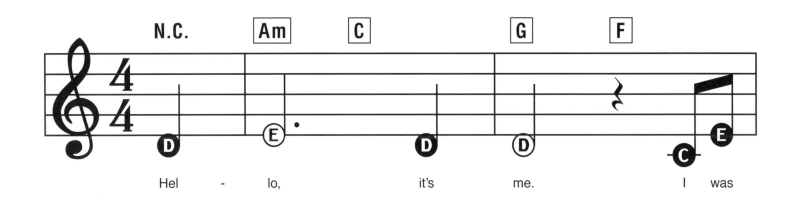

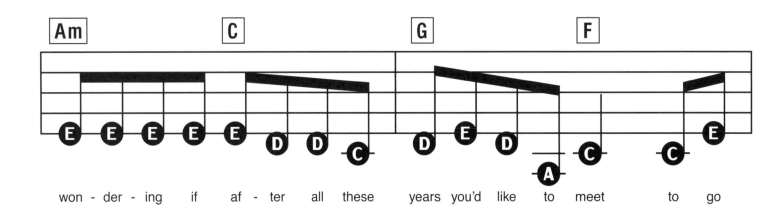

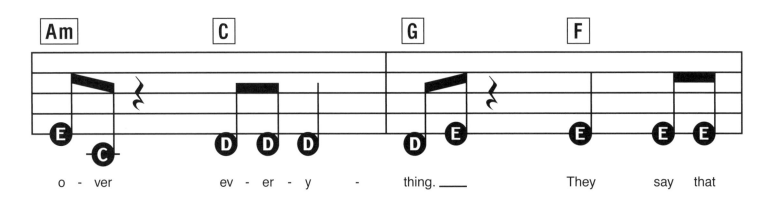

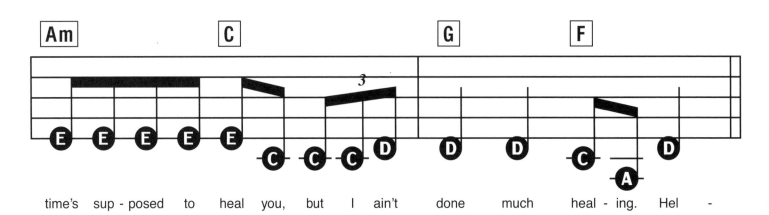

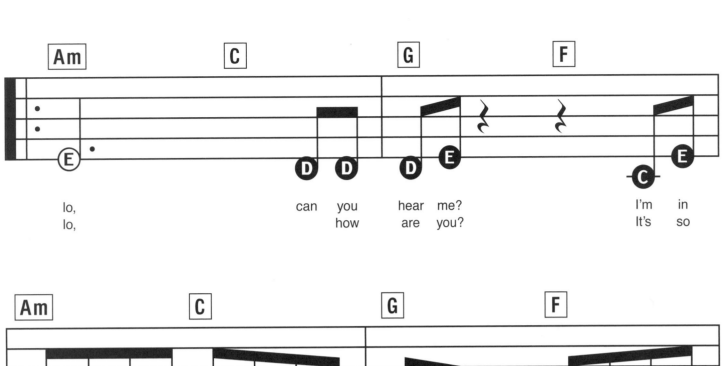

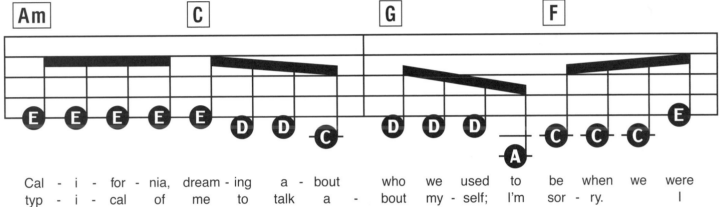

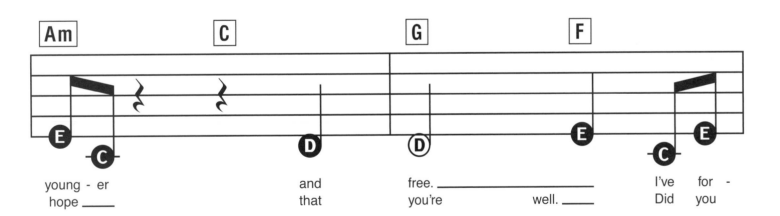

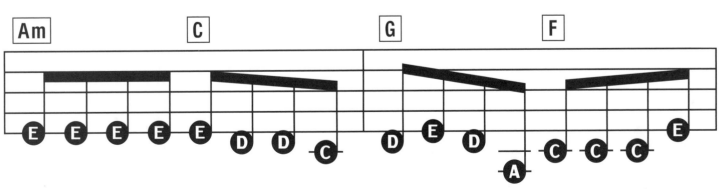

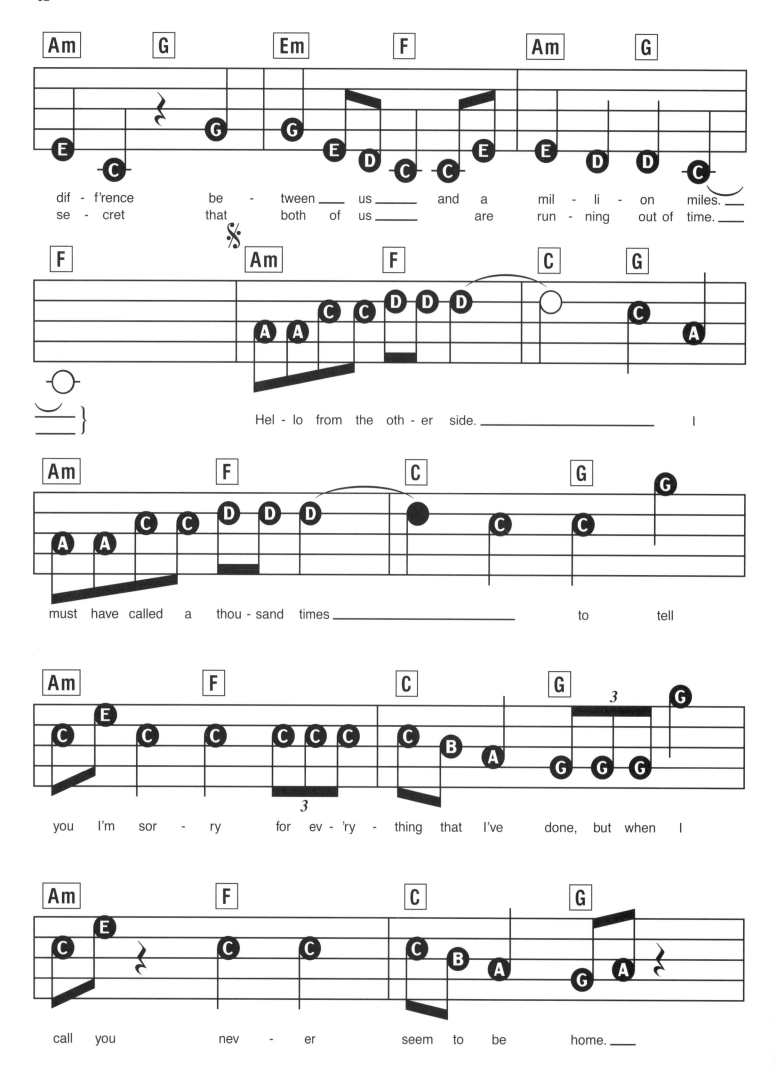

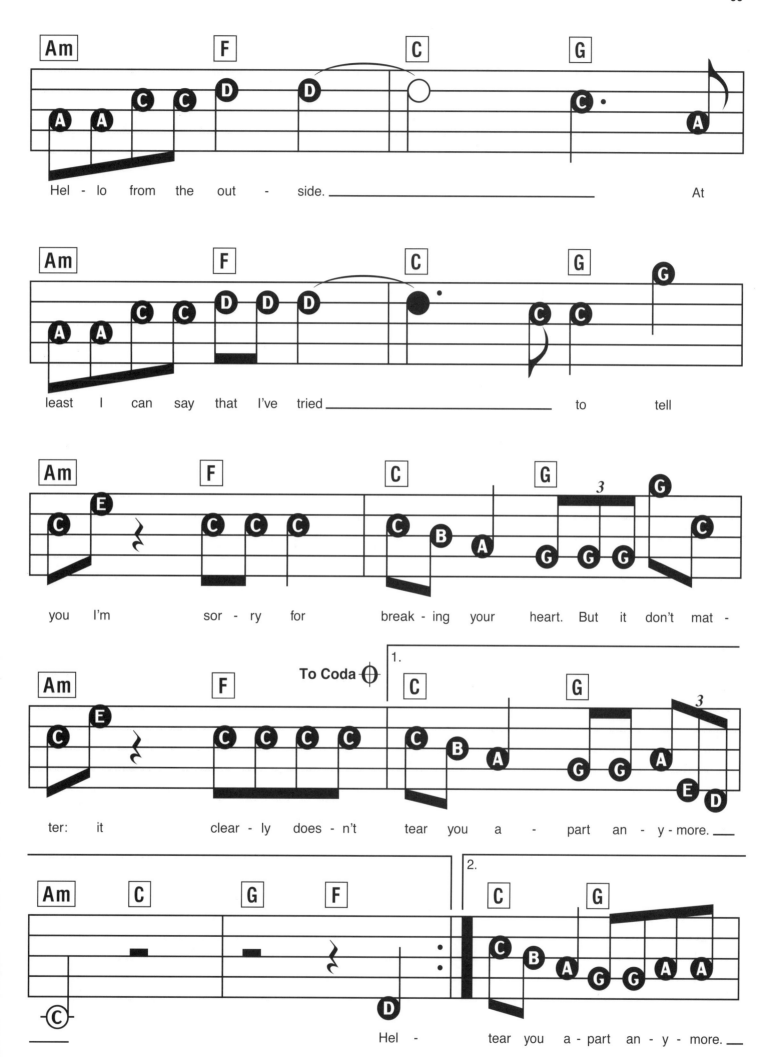

34

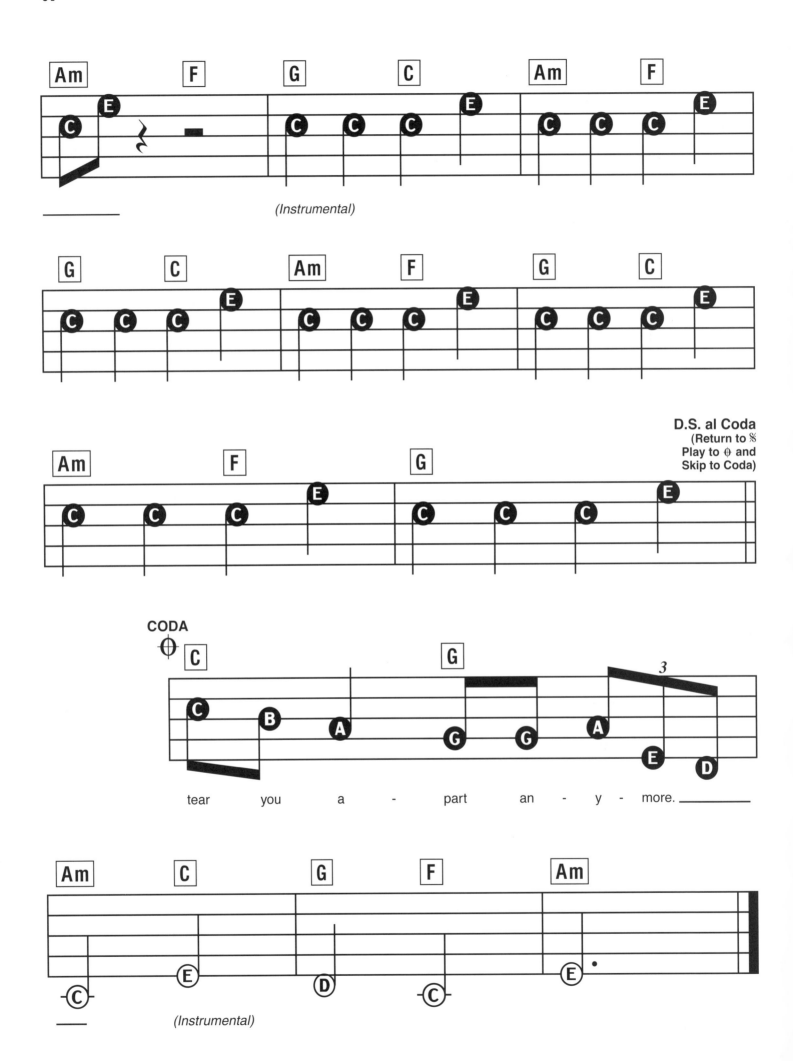

I'm Not the Only One

Registration 8
Rhythm: 8-Beat or Rock

Words and Music by Sam Smith
and James Napier

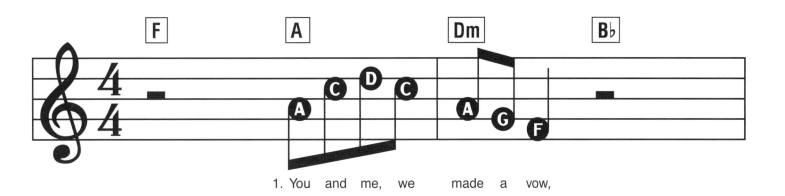

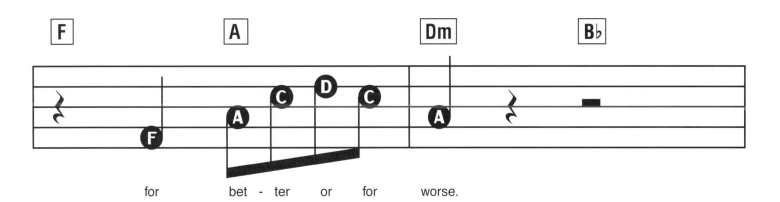

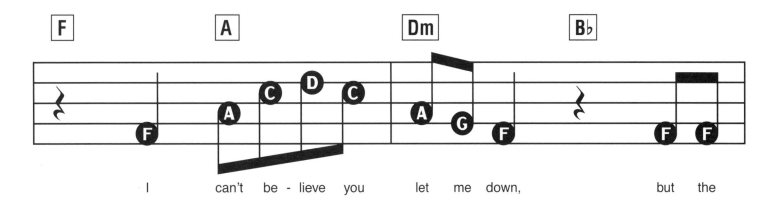

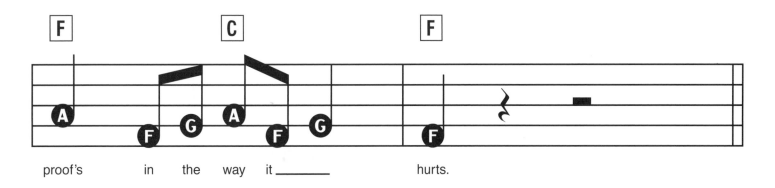

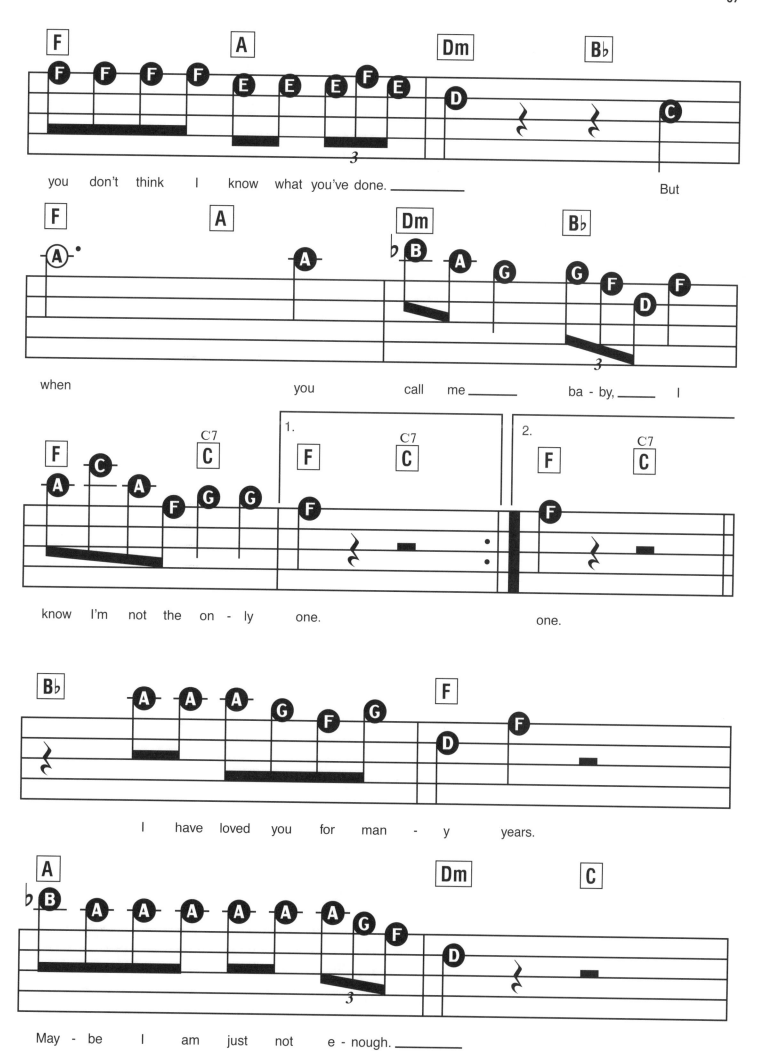

38

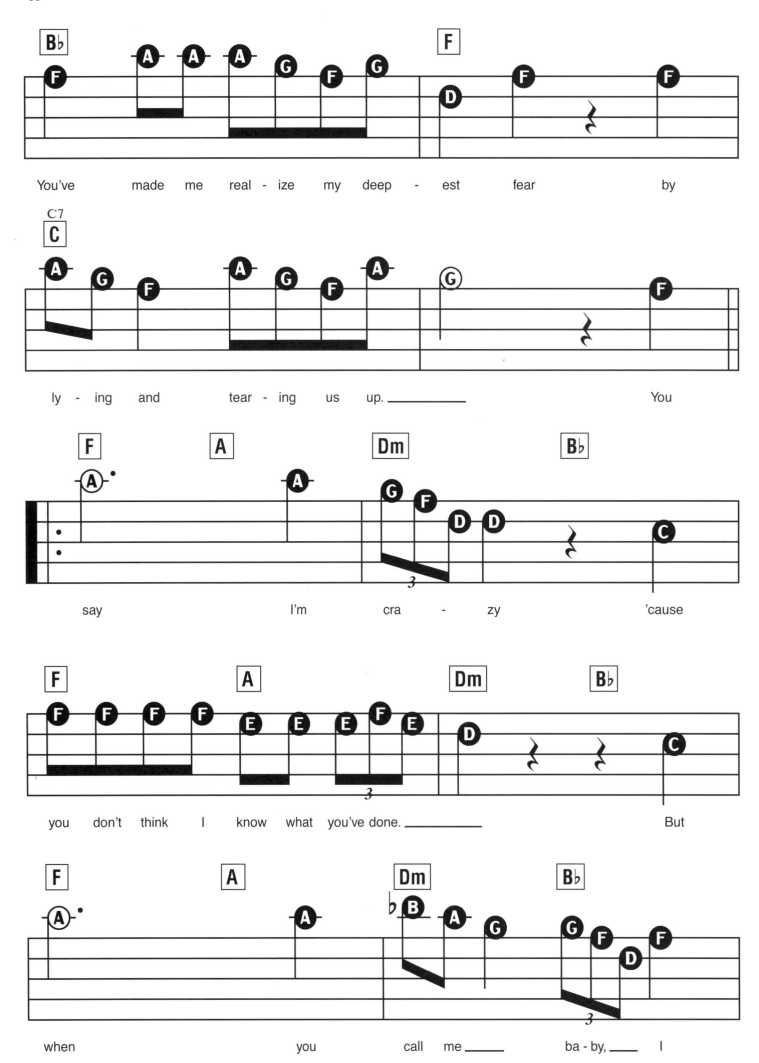

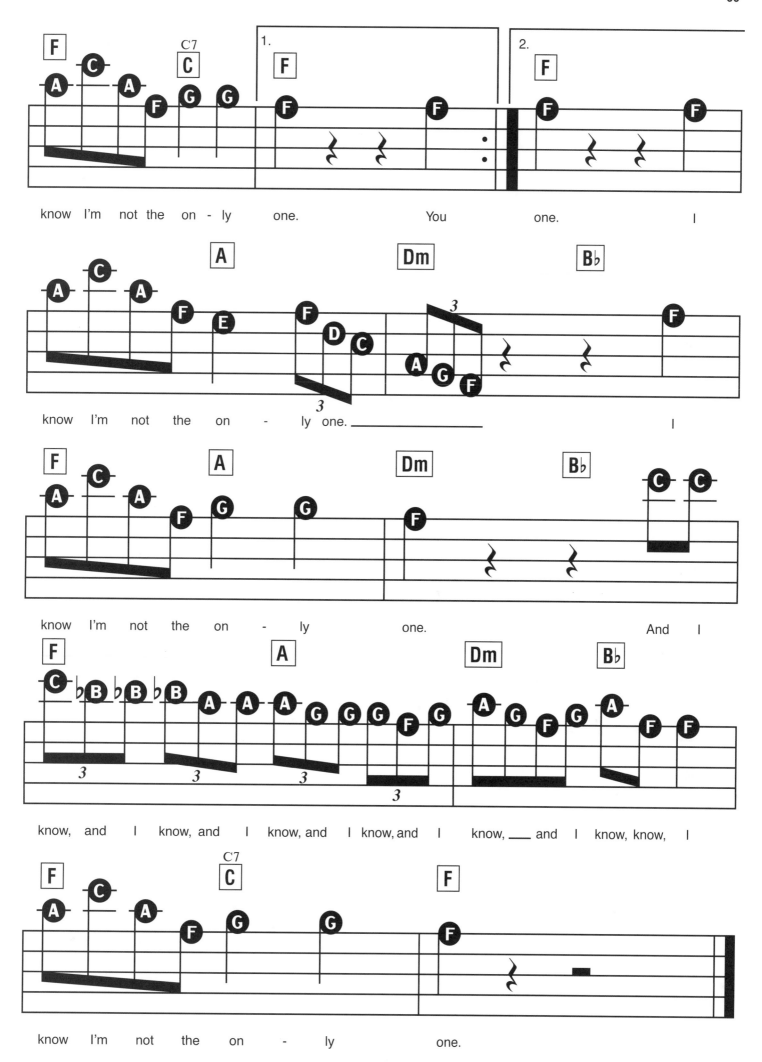

Renegades

Registration 4
Rhythm: Country Pop or Rock

Words and Music by Alexander Junior Grant,
Adam Levin, Casey Harris, Noah Feldshuh
and Sam Harris

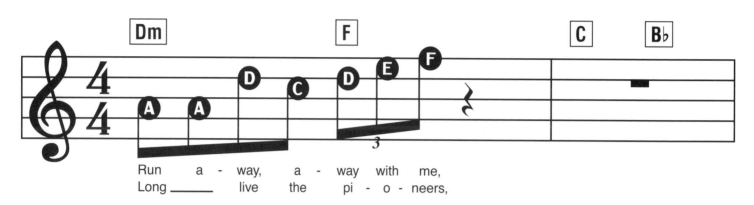

Run a - way, a - way with me,
Long _____ live the pi - o - neers,

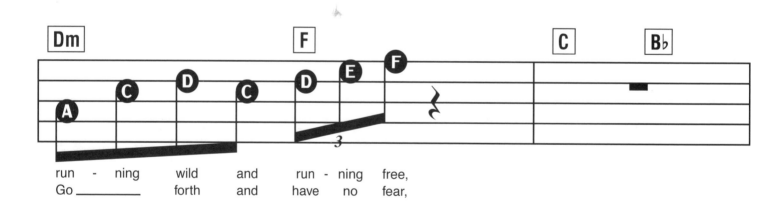

lost souls in rev - el - ry,
reb - els and mu - ti - neers.

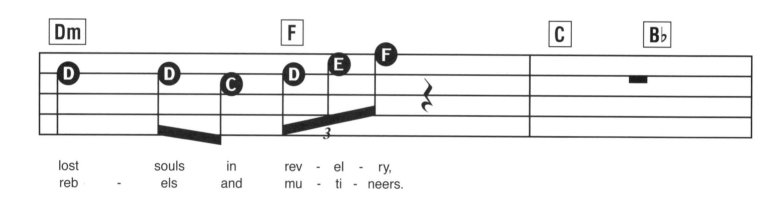

run - ning wild and run - ning free,
Go _____ forth and have no fear,

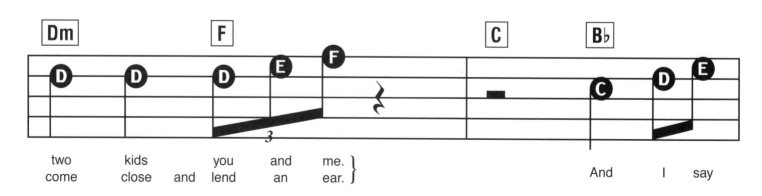

two kids you and me. }
come close and lend an ear.

And I say

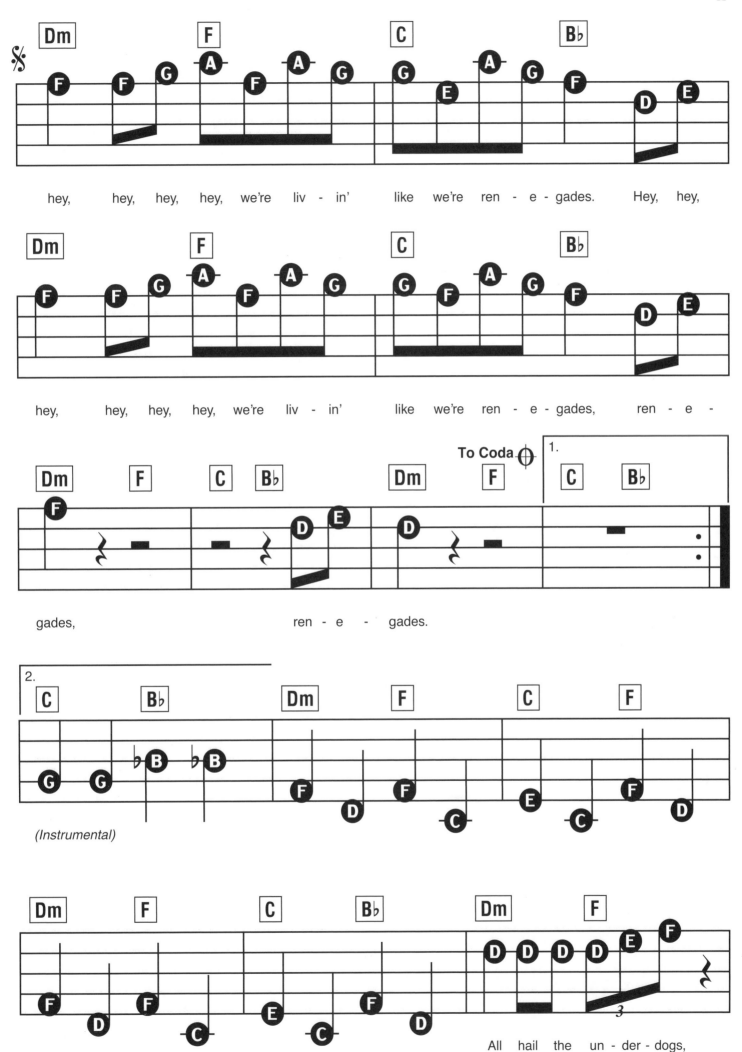

42

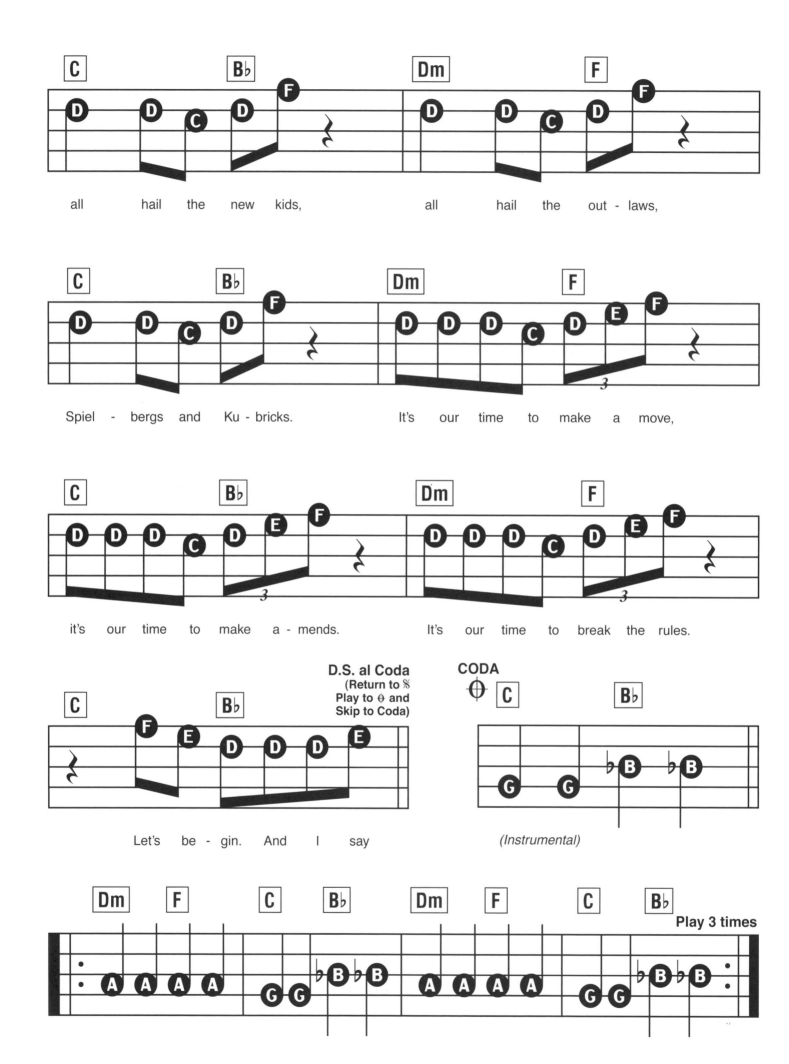

Riptide

Registration 4
Rhythm: Rock or Dance

Words and Music by
Vance Joy

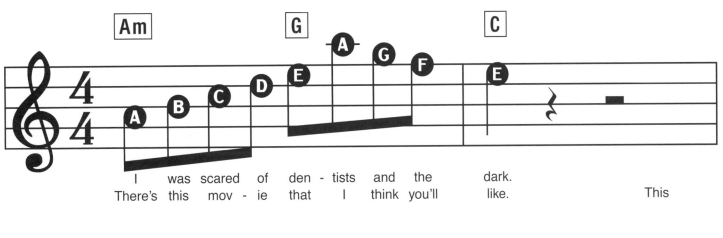

I was scared of den - tists and the dark. This
There's this mov - ie that I think you'll like.

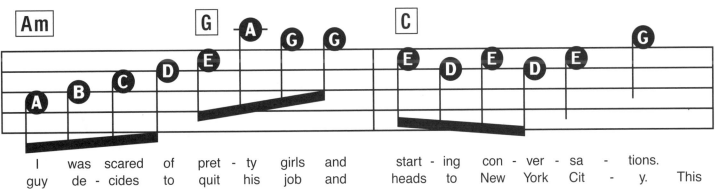

I was scared of pret - ty girls and start - ing con - ver - sa - tions.
guy de - cides to quit his job and heads to New York Cit - y. This

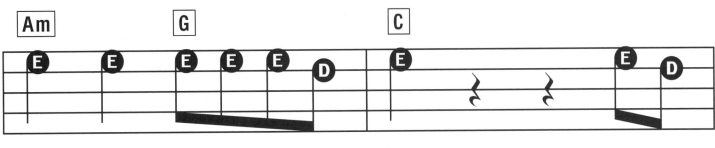

All my friends are turn - ing green; you're the
cow - boy's run - ning from him - self, and

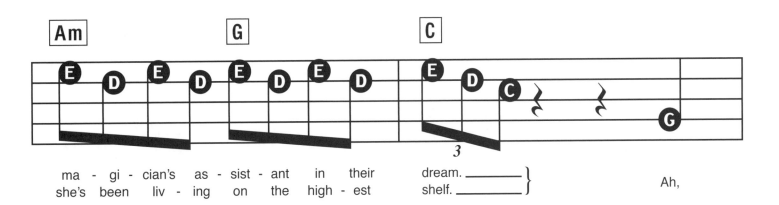

ma - gi - cian's as - sist - ant in their dream. you're the
she's been liv - ing on the high - est shelf. Ah,

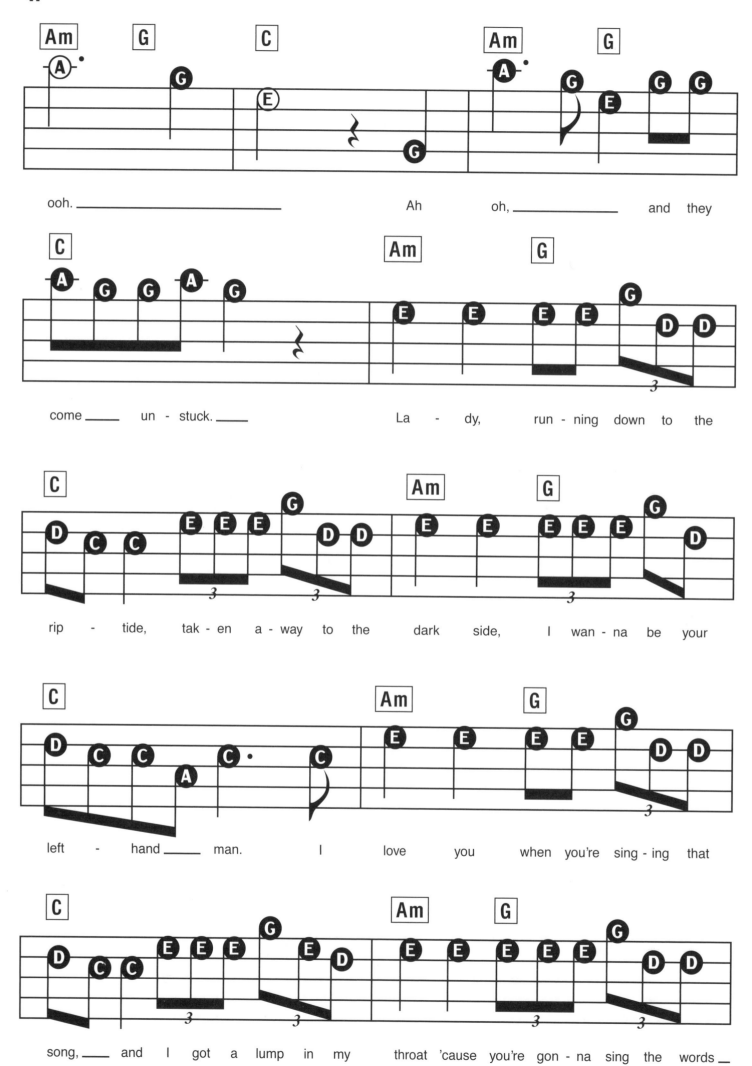

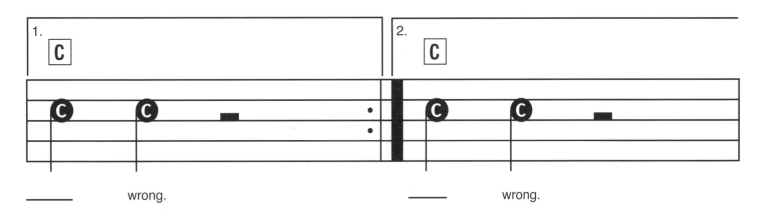

wrong.   wrong.

N.C.

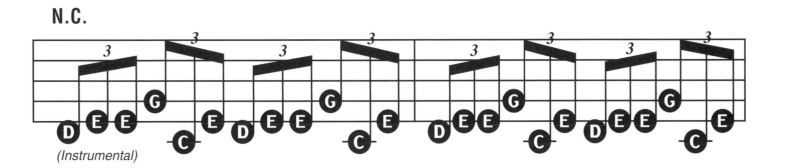

(Instrumental)

Am   **G**

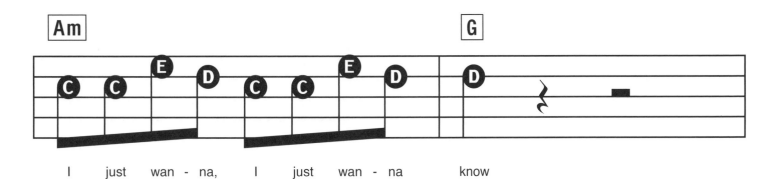

I just wan - na,   I just wan - na   know

C   **F**

if you're gon - na,   if you're gon - na   stay.

Am   **G**

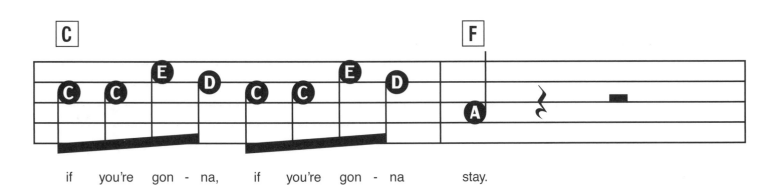

I just got - ta,   I just got - ta   know;

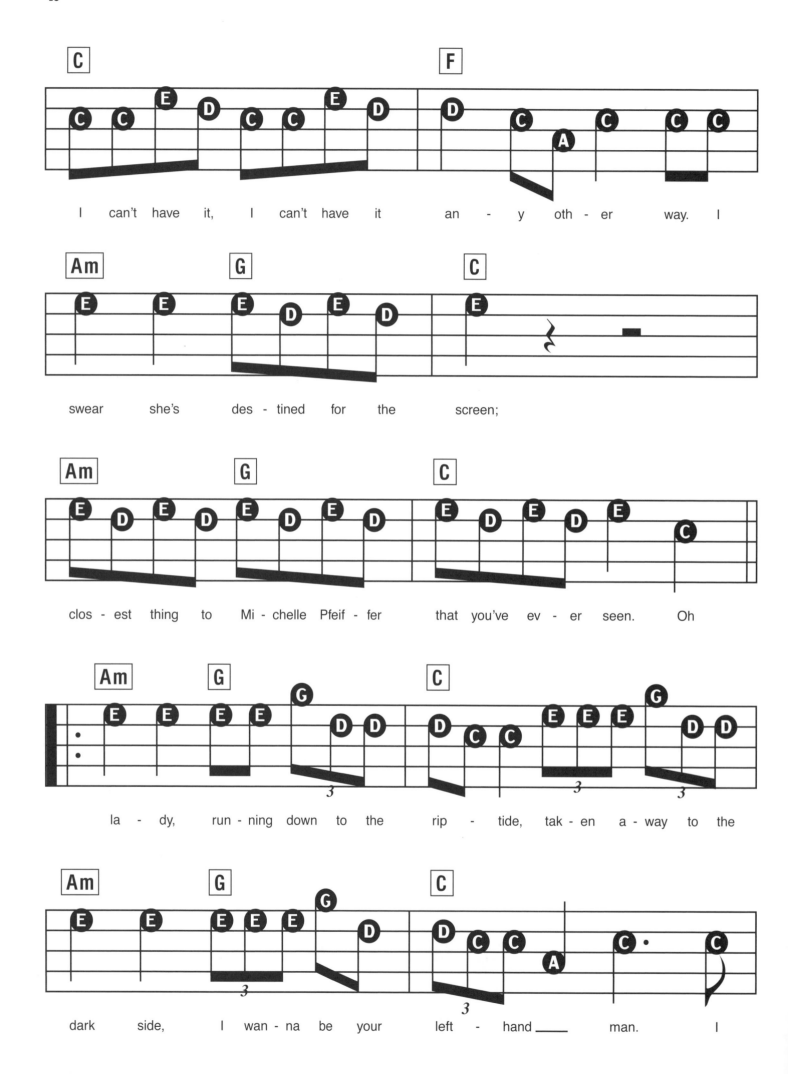

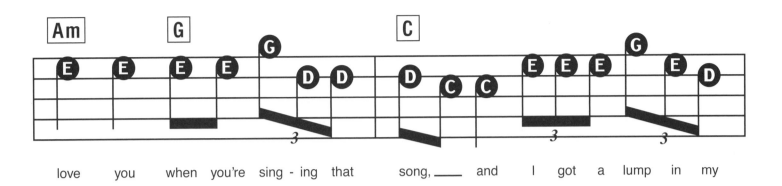

love you when you're sing - ing that song, _____ and I got a lump in my

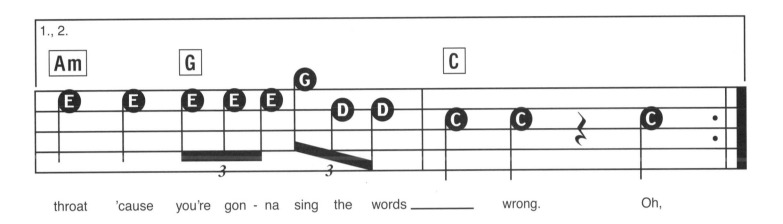

1., 2.

throat 'cause you're gon - na sing the words _____ wrong.   Oh,

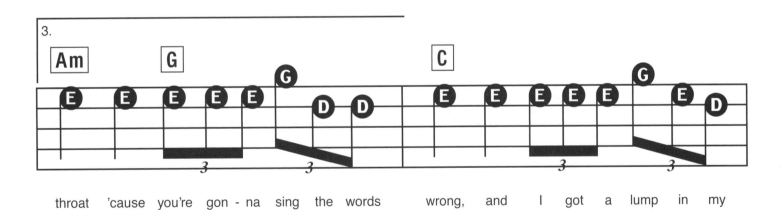

3.

throat 'cause you're gon - na sing the words   wrong, and I got a lump in my

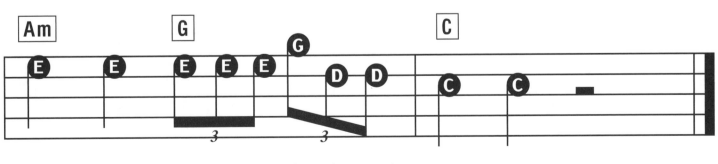

throat 'cause you're gon - na sing the words _____ wrong.

Shake It Off

Registration 9
Rhythm: Pop or Dance

Words and Music by Taylor Swift,
Max Martin and Shellback

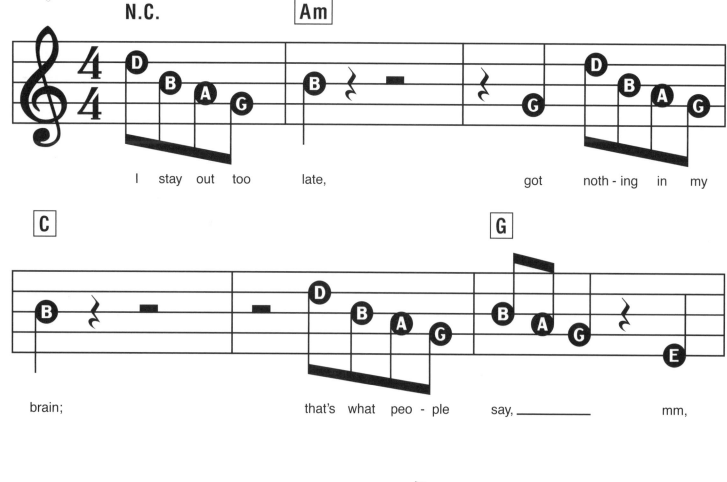

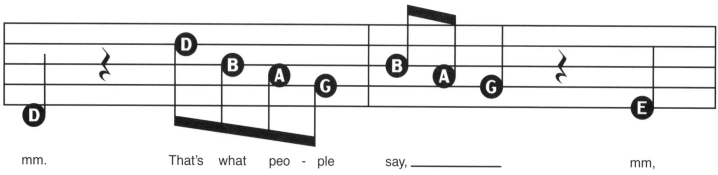

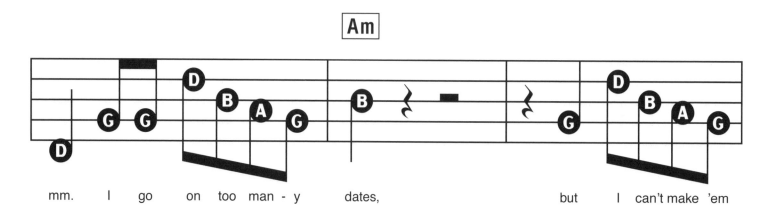

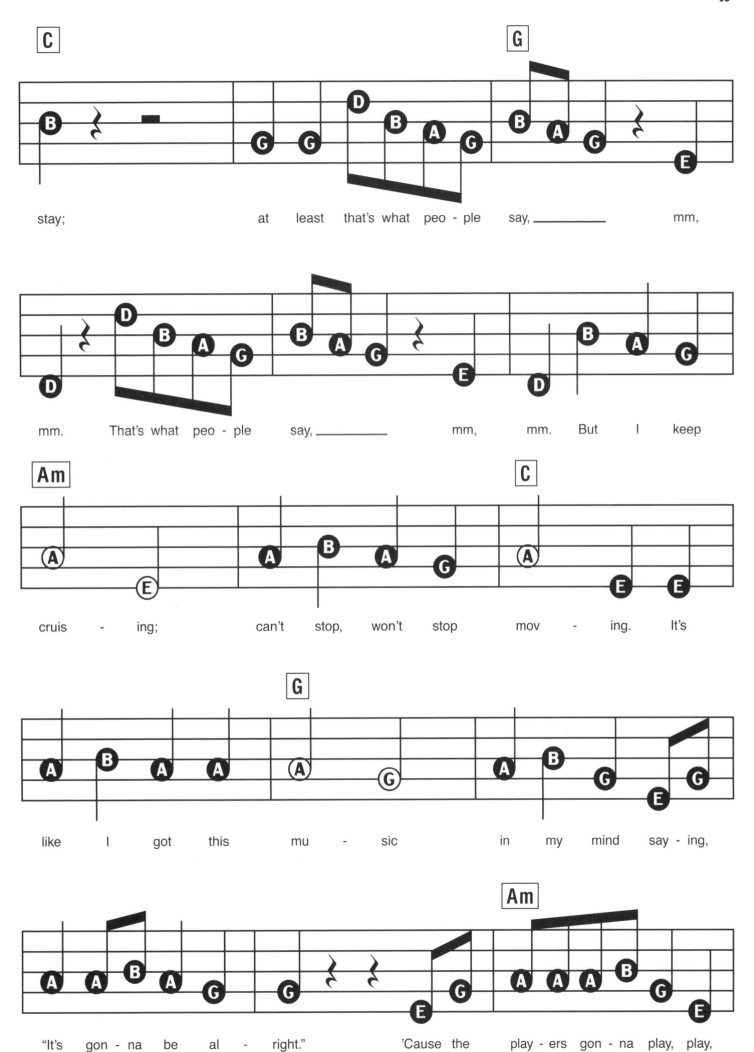

50

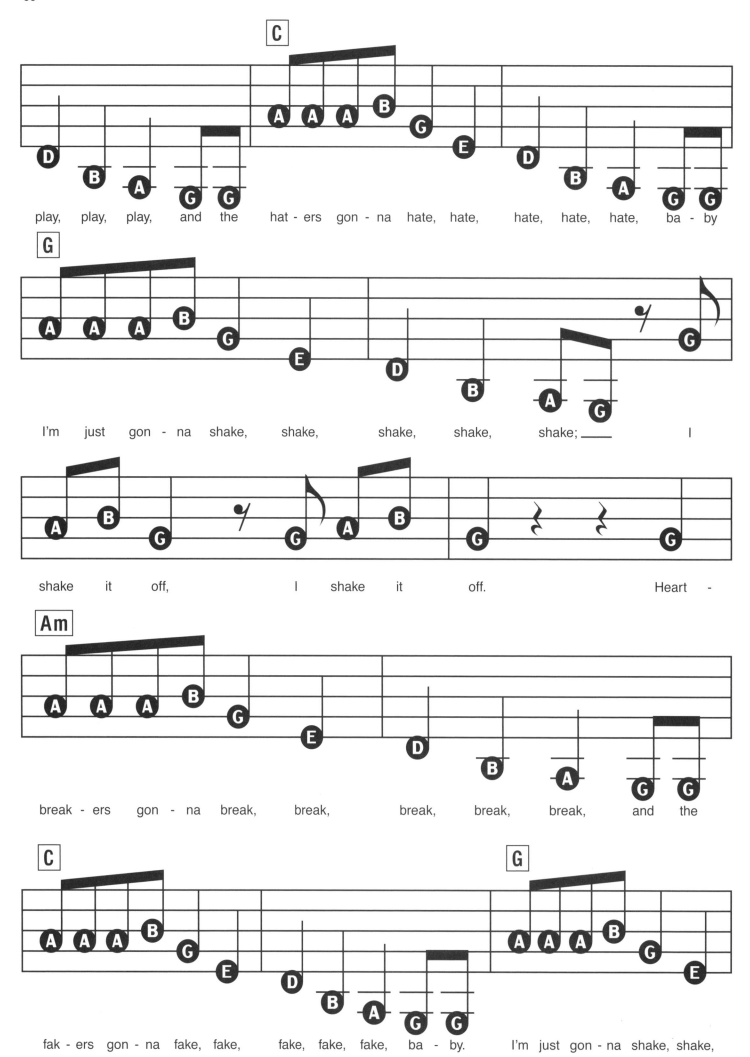

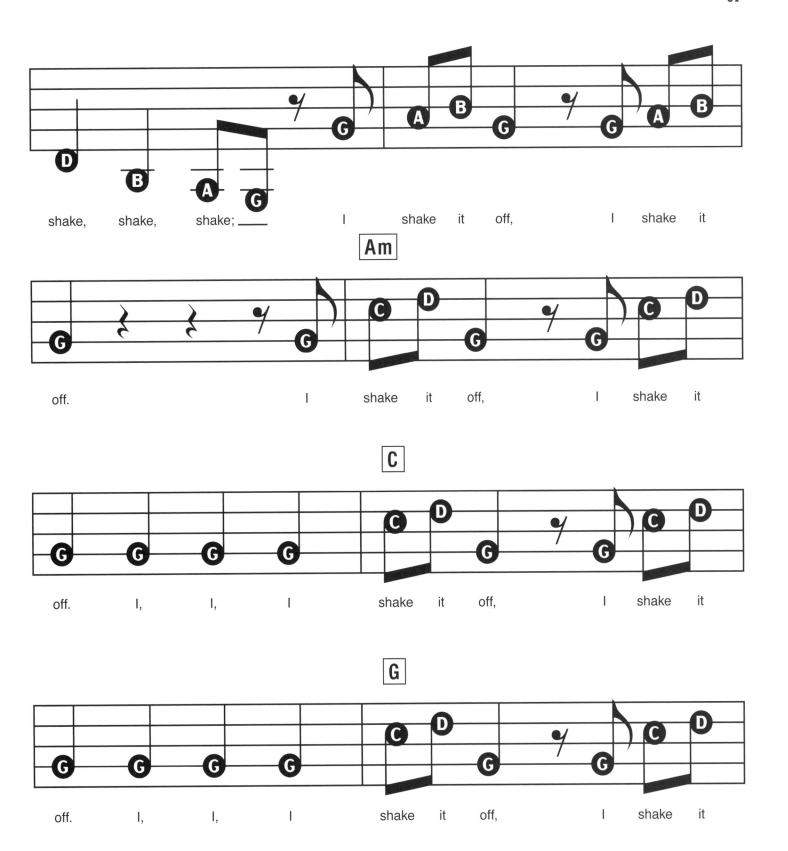

shake,   shake,   shake; _____   I   shake   it   off,   I   shake   it

Am

off.   I   shake   it   off,   I   shake   it

C

off.   I,   I,   I   shake   it   off,   I   shake   it

G

off.   I,   I,   I   shake   it   off,   I   shake   it

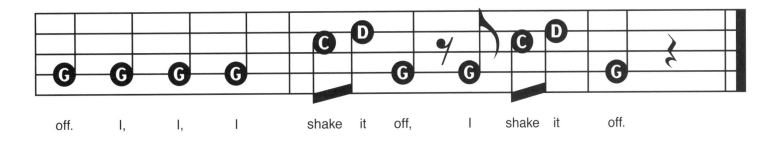

off.   I,   I,   I   shake   it   off,   I   shake   it   off.

Stressed Out

Registration 1
Rhythm: 8-Beat or Rock

Words and Music by
Tyler Joseph

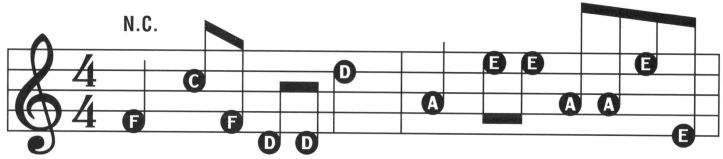

Rap 1: *(See additional lyrics)*

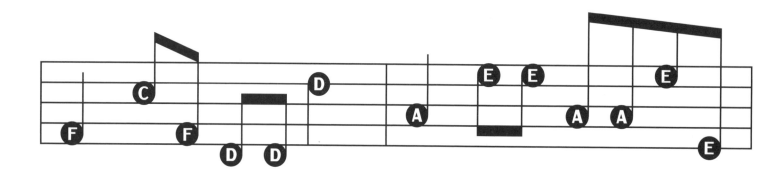

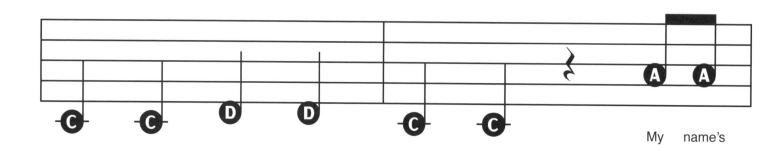

My name's

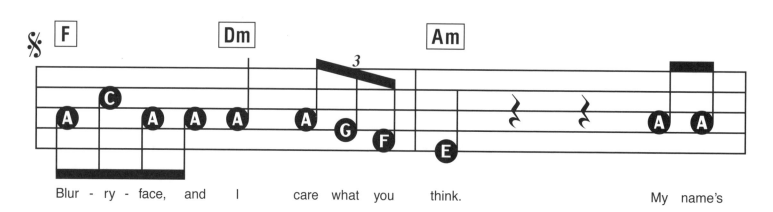

Blur - ry - face, and I care what you think.

My name's

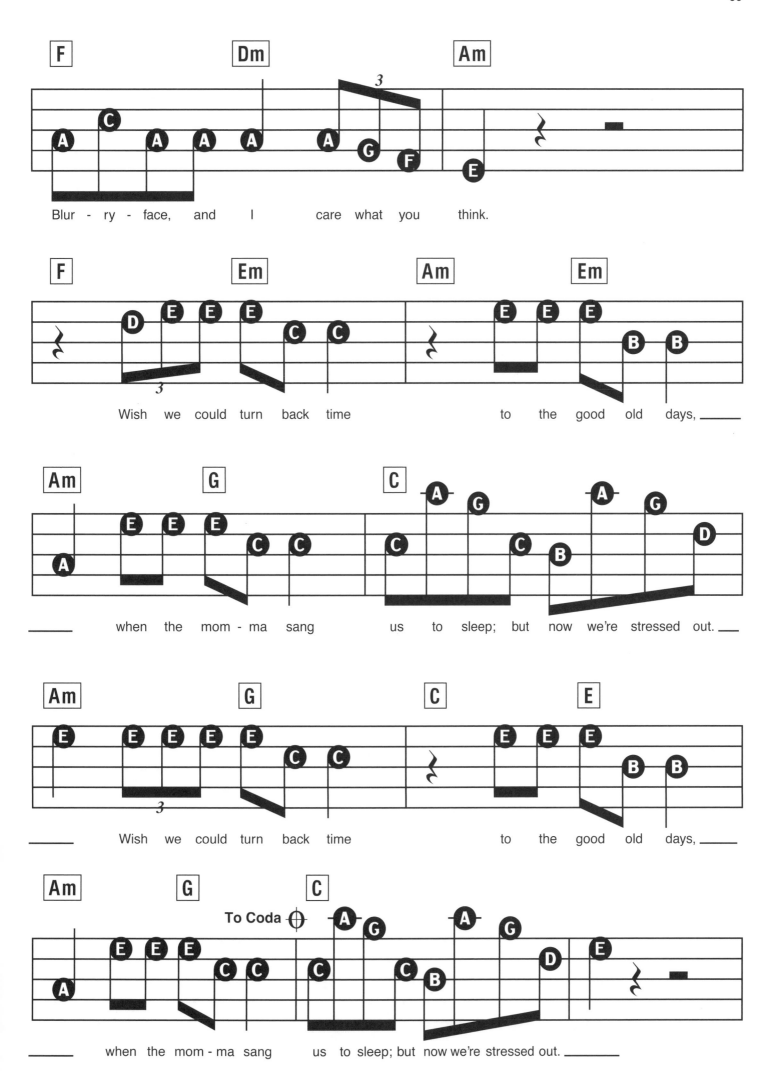

We're   stressed   out. _____

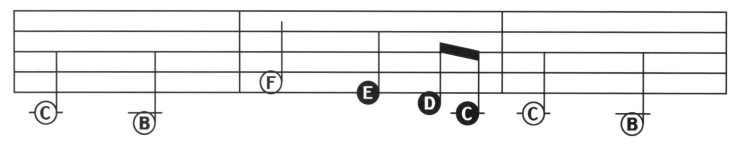

Rap 2: *(See additional lyrics)*

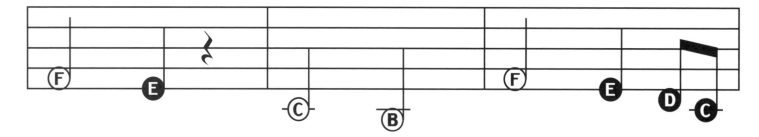

D.S. al Coda
(Return to 𝄋
Play to ⊕ and
Skip to Coda)

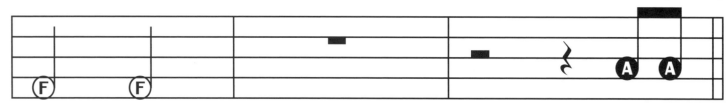

My   name's

CODA
⊕ C

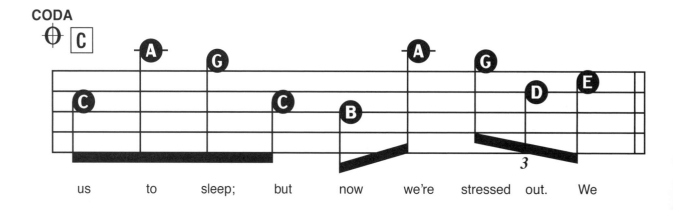

us   to   sleep;   but   now   we're   stressed   out.   We

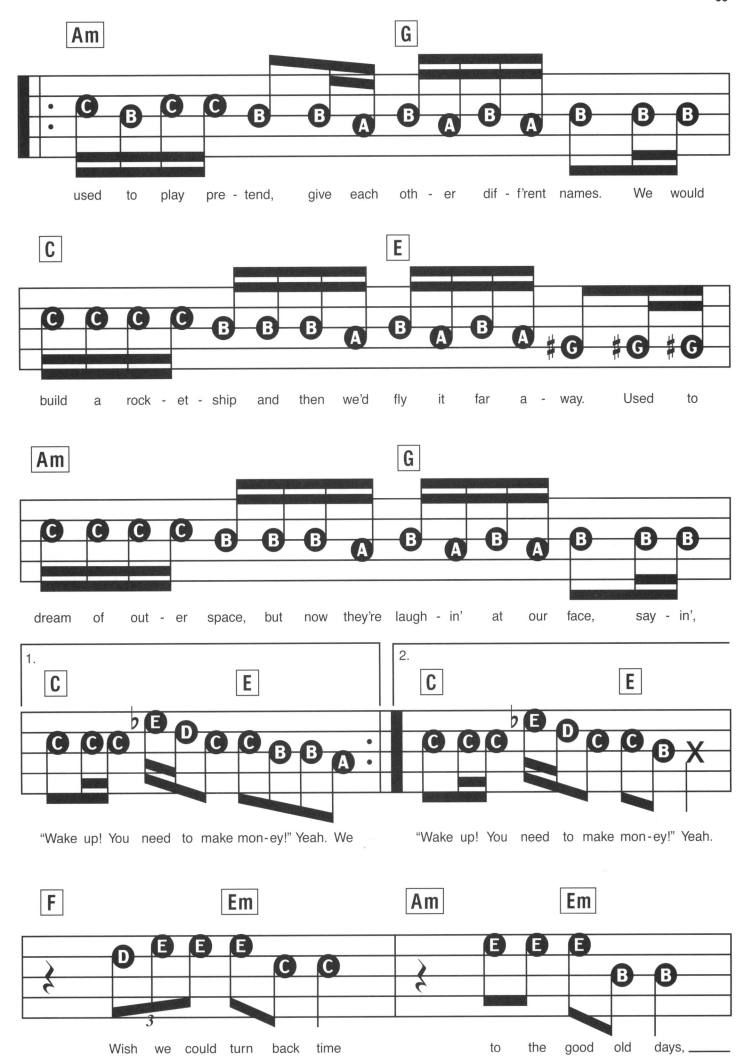

56

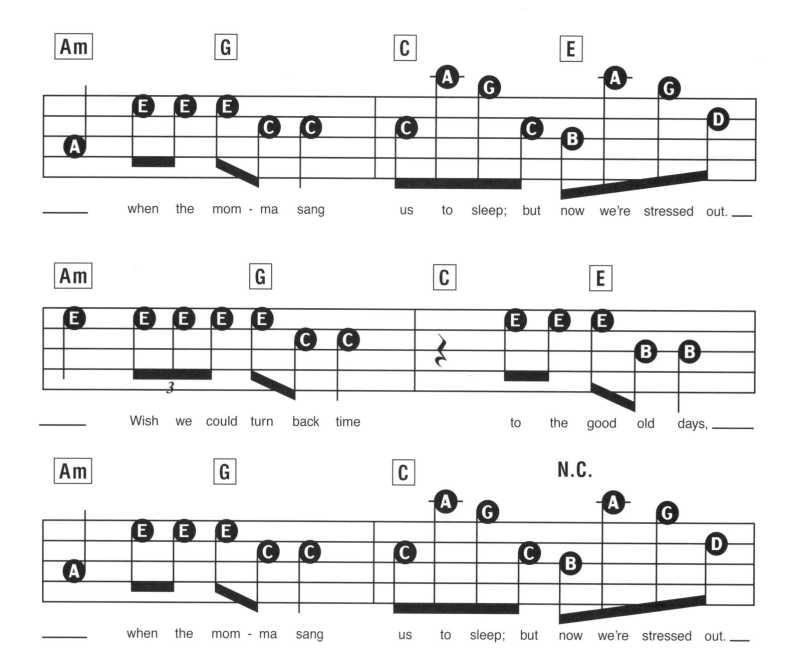

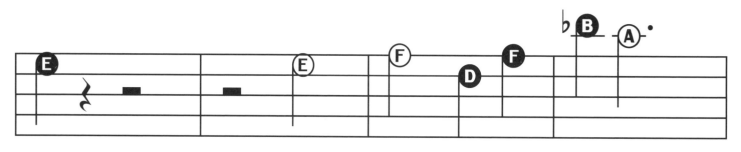

Rap 3: *(See additional lyrics)*

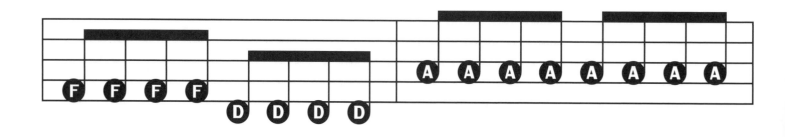

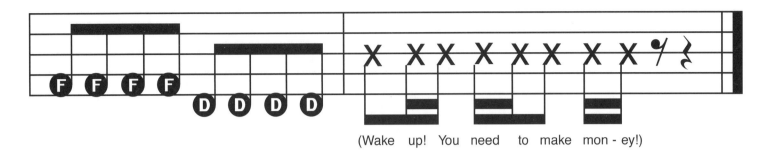

(Wake up! You need to make mon - ey!)

Additional Lyrics

Rap 1: I wish I found some better sounds no one's ever heard.
I wish I had a better voice that sang some better words.
I wish I found some chords in an order that is new.
I wish I didn't have to rhyme every time I sang.

I was told when I get older all my fears would shrink,
But now I'm insecure and I care what people think.

Rap 2: Sometimes a certain smell will take me back to when I was young.
How come I'm never able to identify where it's coming from?
I'd make a candle out of it if I ever found it,
Try to sell it, never sell out of it. I'd probably only sell one.

It'd be to my brother, 'cause we have the same nose,
Same clothes, homegrown, a stone's throw from a creek we used to roam.
But it would remind us of when nothing really mattered.
Out of student loans and treehouse homes, we all would take the latter.

Rap 3: We used to play pretend, used to play pretend, bunny.
We used to play pretend; wake up, you need the money.
We used to play pretend, used to play pretend, bunny.
We used to play pretend; wake up, you need the money.

We used to play pretend, give each other different names;
We would build a rocket ship and then we'd fly it far away.
Used to dream of outer space, but now they're laughing at our face,
Saying, "Wake up, you need to make money!" Yo.

A Sky Full of Stars

Registration 8
Rhythm: Dance or Rock

Words and Music by Guy Berryman,
Jon Buckland, Will Champion,
Chris Martin and Tim Bergling

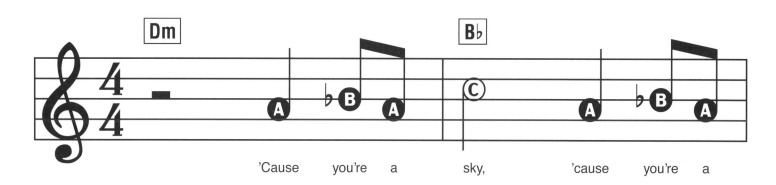

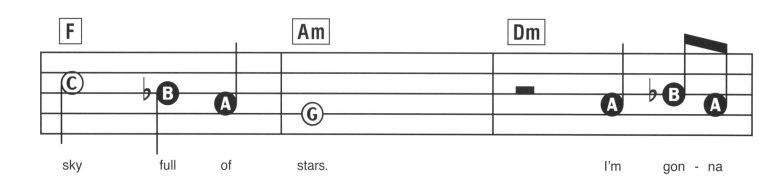

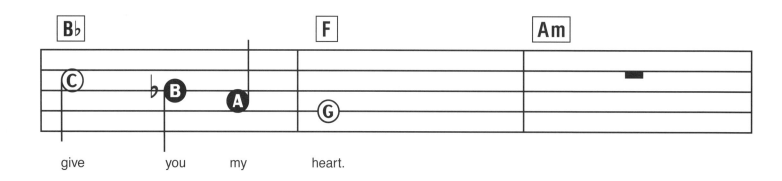

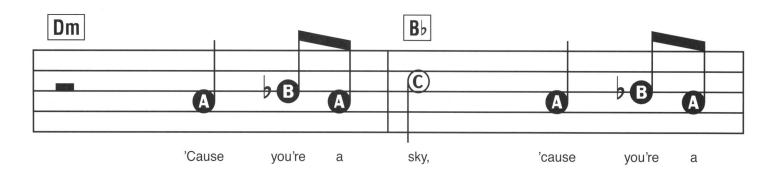

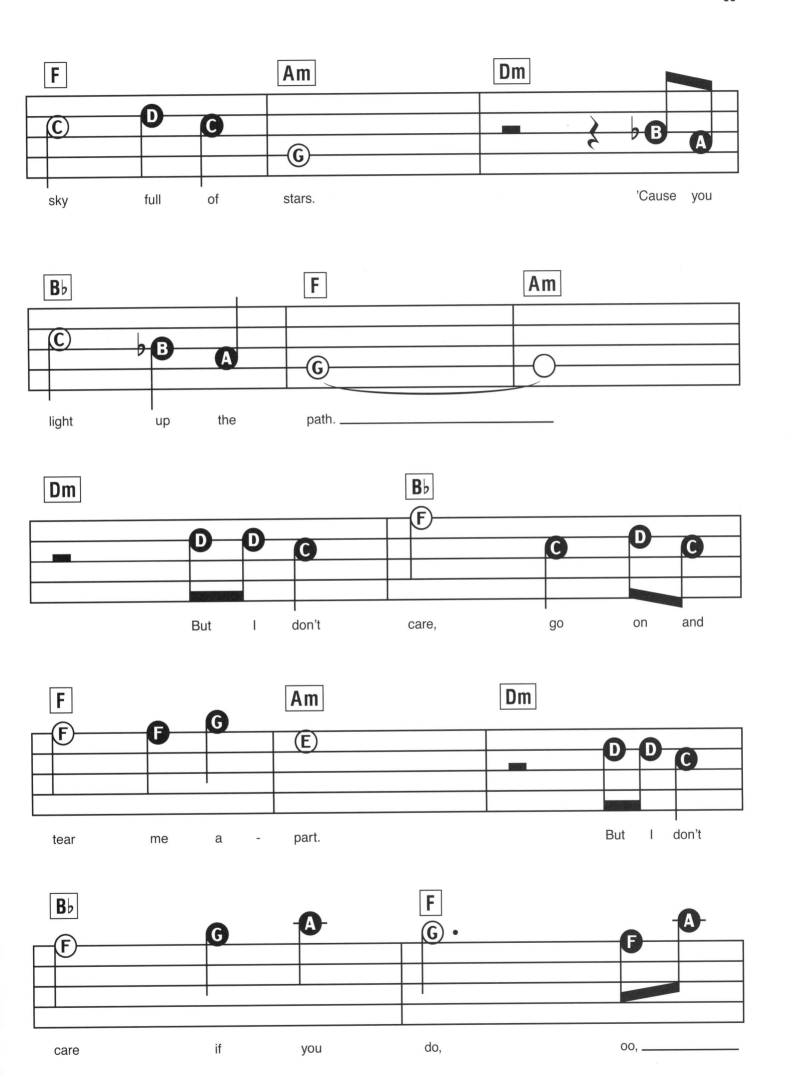

59

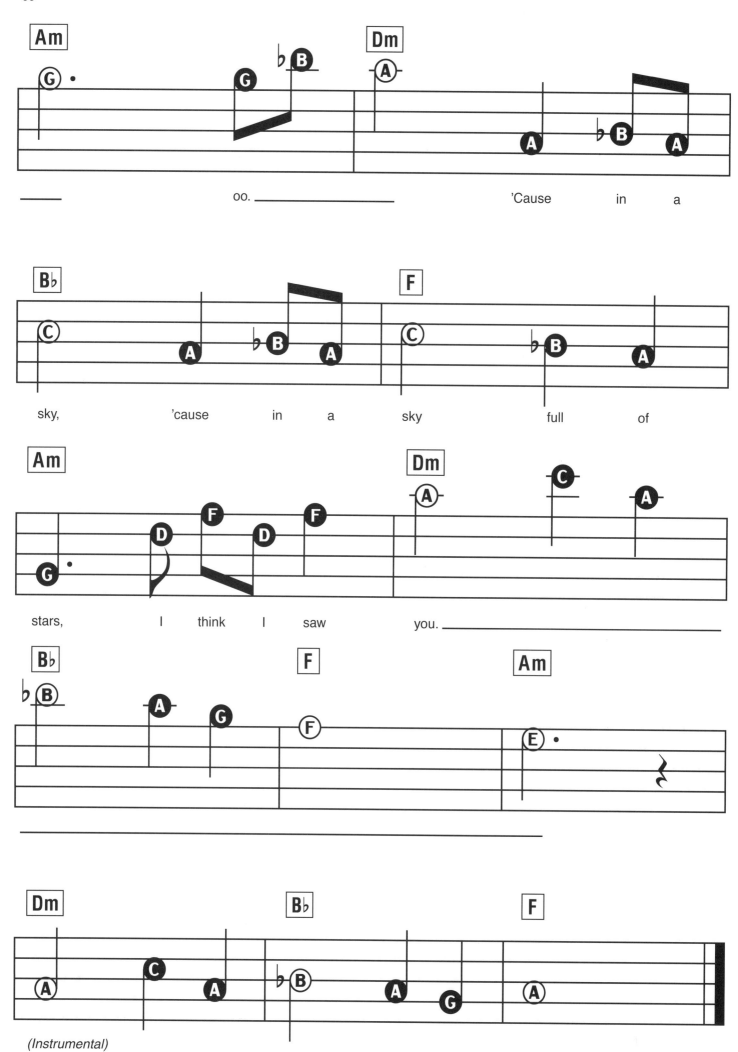

oo. _____ 'Cause in a sky, 'cause in a sky full of stars, I think I saw you. _____

(Instrumental)

Take Me to Church

Registration 1
Rhythm: None

Words and Music by
Andrew Hozier-Byrne

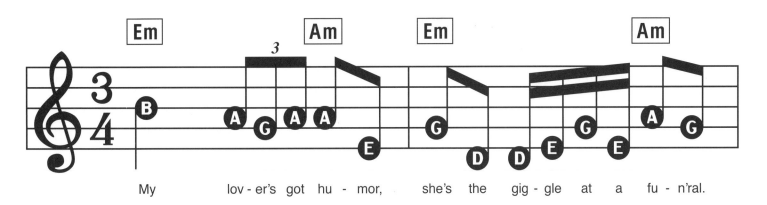

My lov - er's got hu - mor, she's the gig - gle at a fu - n'ral.

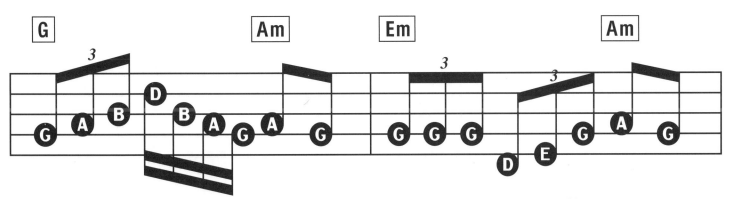

Knows ev - 'ry - bod - y's dis - ap - pro - val, I should - 've wor - shipped her soon - er.

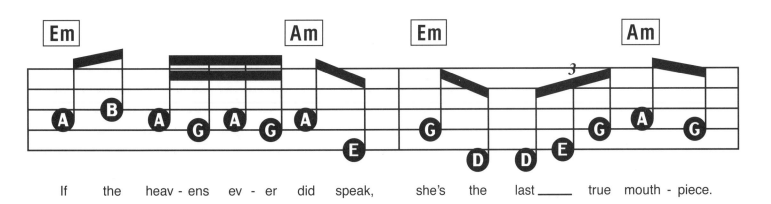

If the heav - ens ev - er did speak, she's the last _____ true mouth - piece.

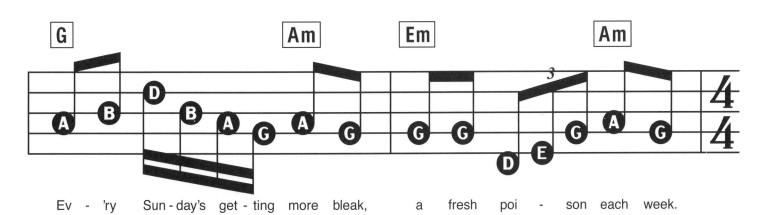

Ev - 'ry Sun - day's get - ting more bleak, a fresh poi - son each week.

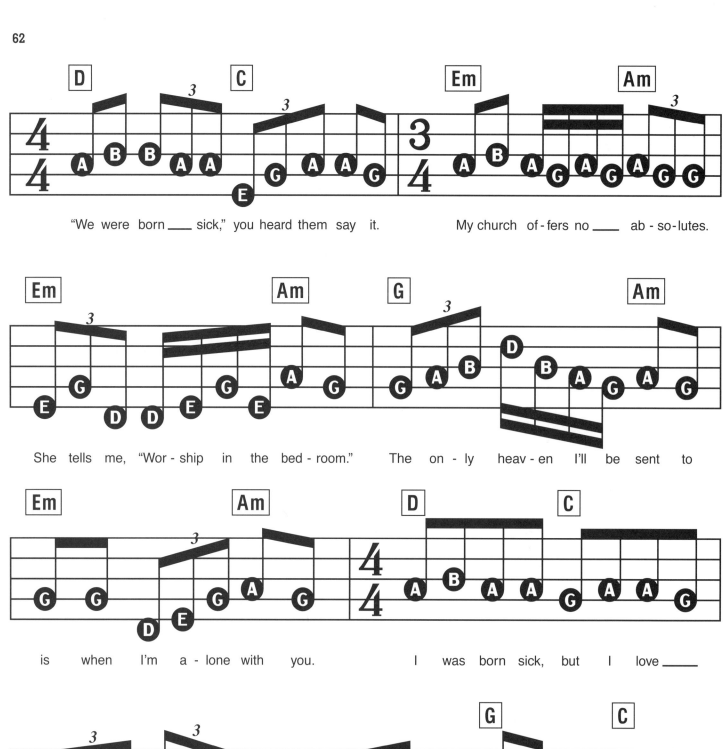

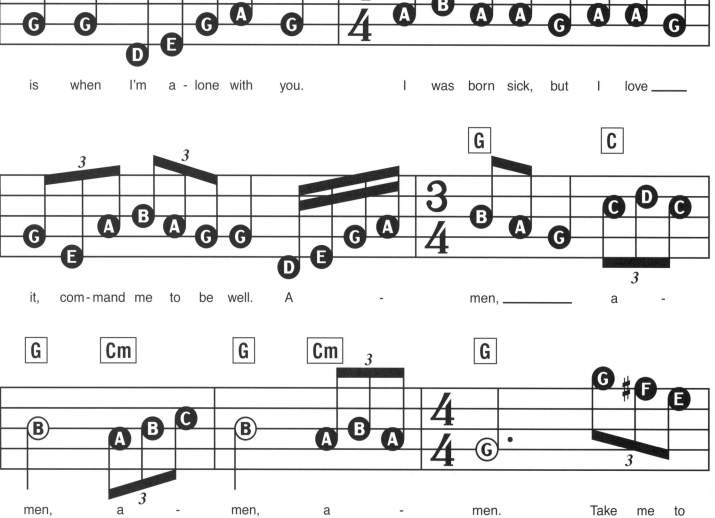

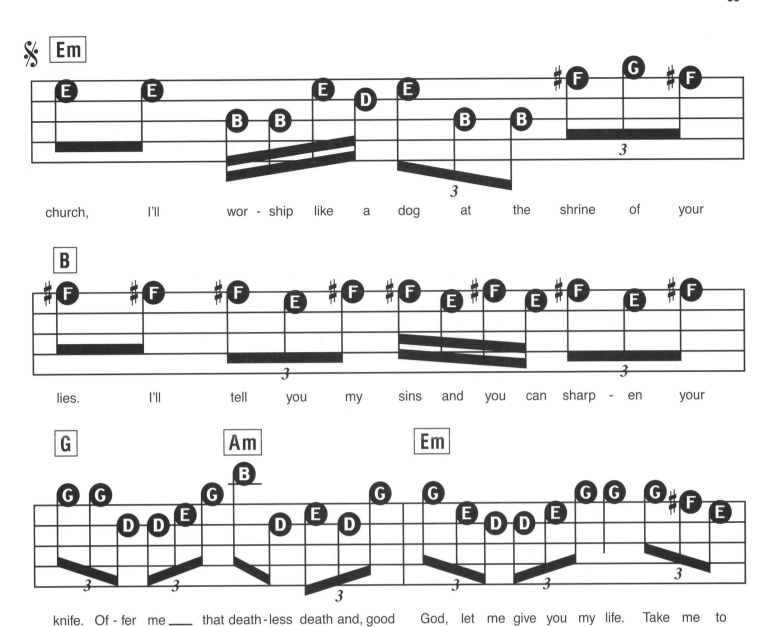

church, I'll wor - ship like a dog at the shrine of your

lies. I'll tell you my sins and you can sharp - en your

knife. Of - fer me ___ that death - less death and, good God, let me give you my life. Take me to

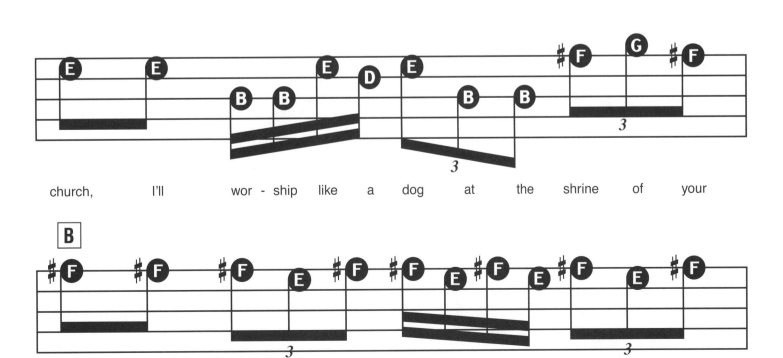

church, I'll wor - ship like a dog at the shrine of your

lies, I'll tell you my sins and you can sharp - en your

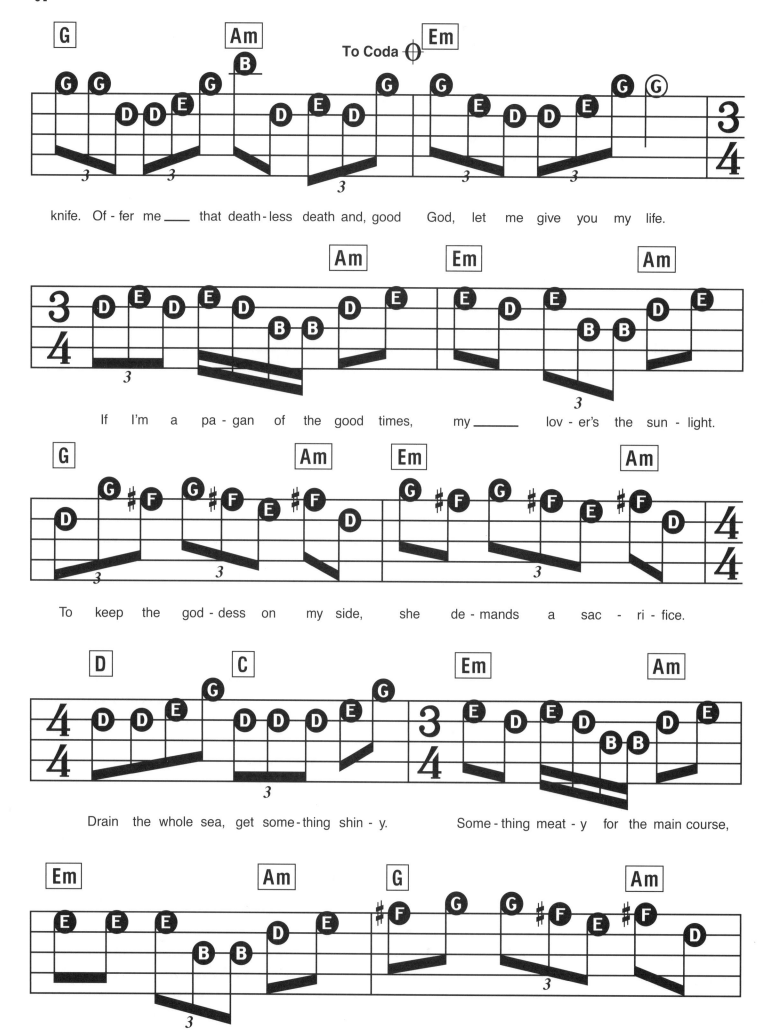

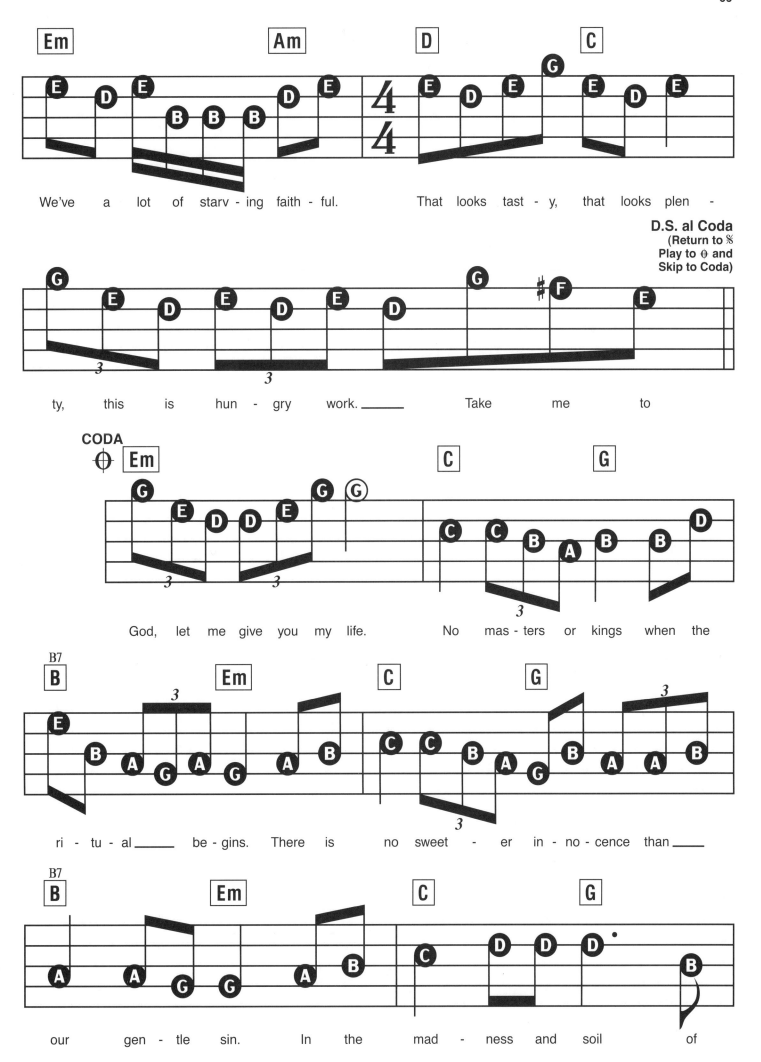

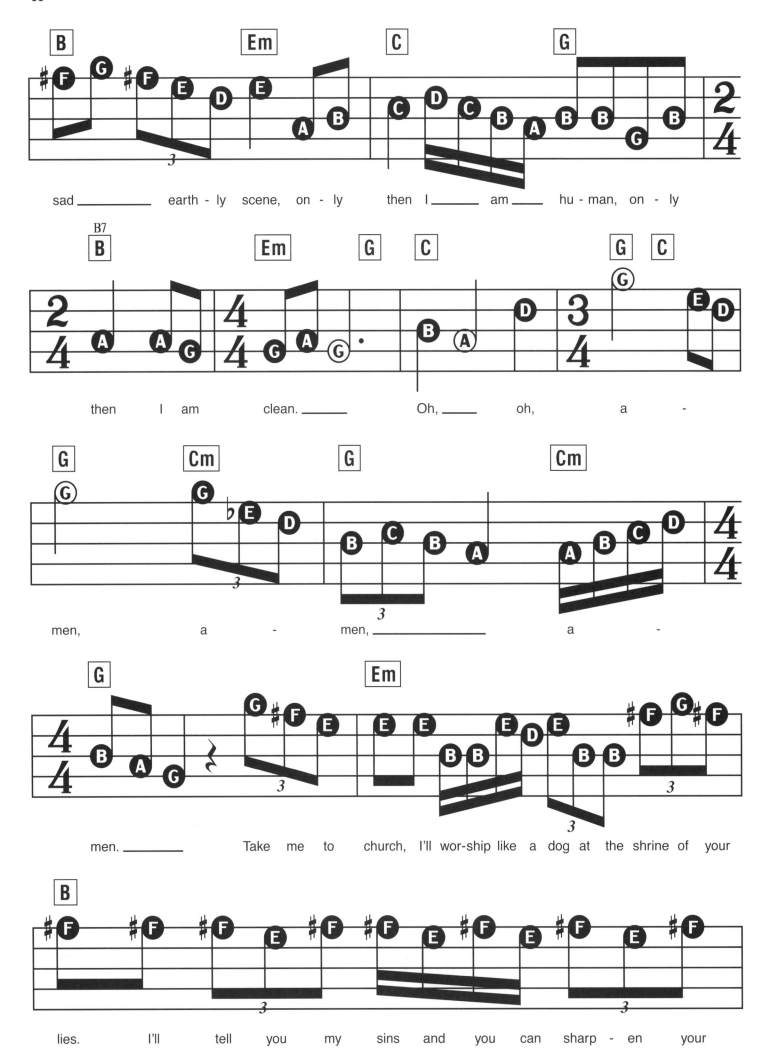

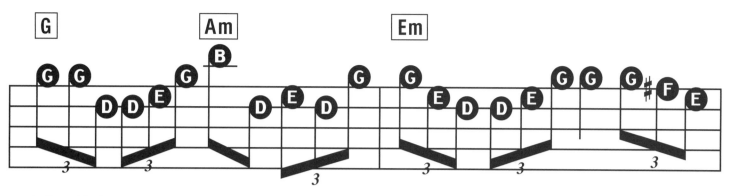

knife. Of - fer me ___ that death - less death and, good God, let me give you my life. Take me to

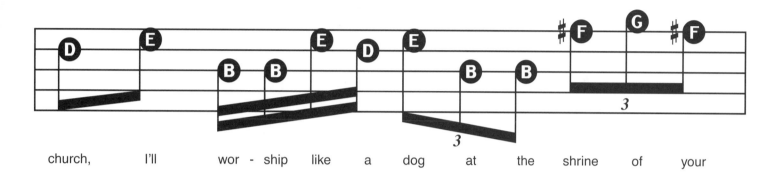

church, I'll wor - ship like a dog at the shrine of your

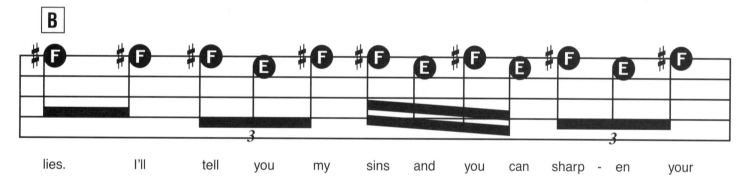

lies. I'll tell you my sins and you can sharp - en your

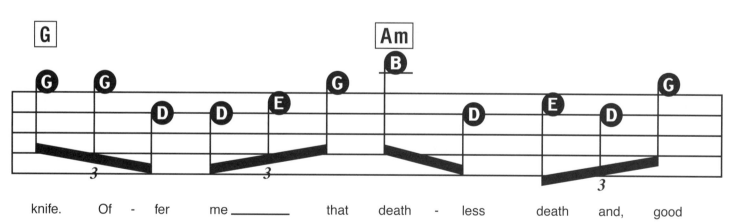

knife. Of - fer me ___ that death - less death and, good

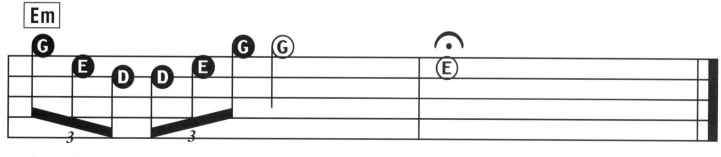

God, let me give you my life. ___

Thinking Out Loud

Registration 4
Rhythm: 8-Beat or Rock

Words and Music by Ed Sheeran
and Amy Wadge

When your legs don't work like they used to be - fore
When my hair's all but gone and my mem - o - ry fades,

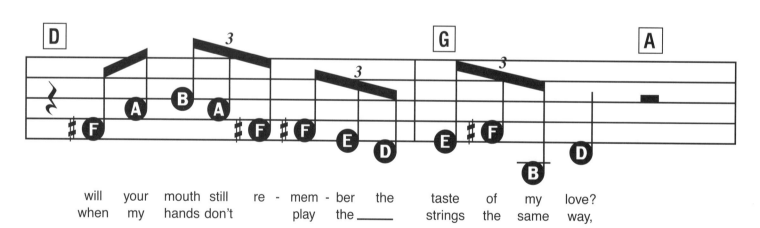

and I can't sweep you off of your feet,
and the crowds don't re - mem - ber my name,

will your mouth still re - mem - ber the taste of my love?
when my hands don't play the ___ strings the same way,

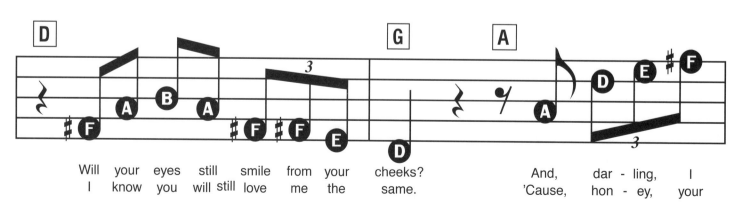

Will your eyes still smile from your cheeks? And, dar - ling, I
I know you will still love me the same. 'Cause, hon - ey, your

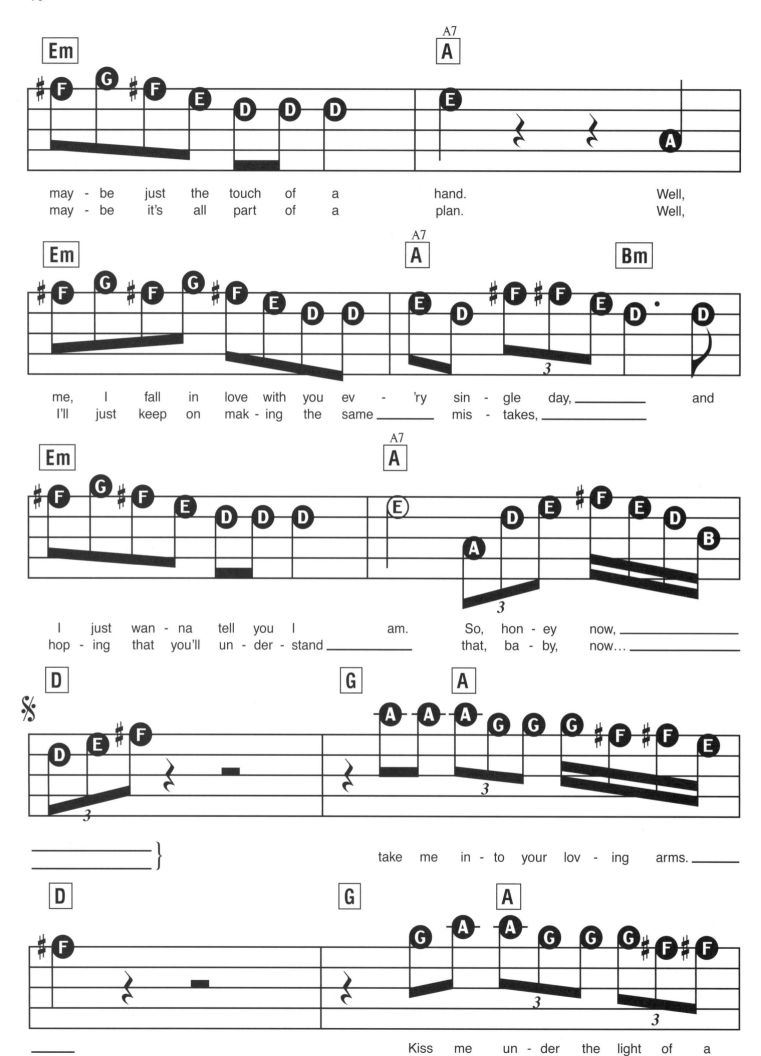

72

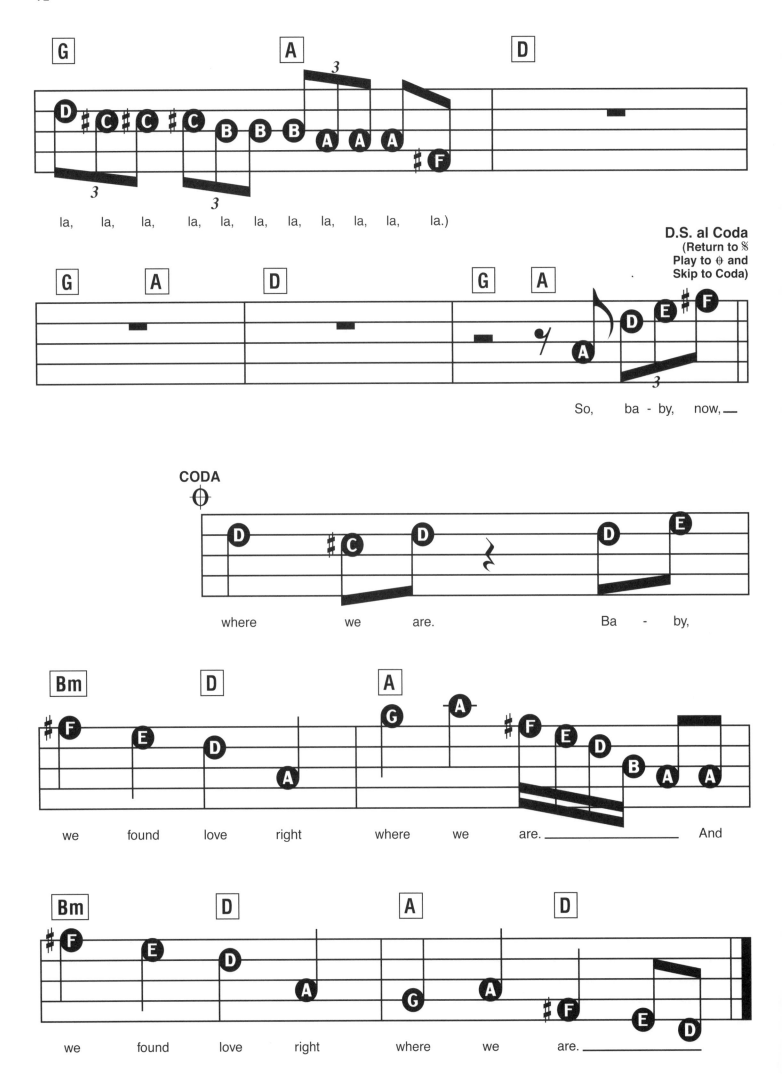

Uptown Funk

Registration 2
Rhythm: Funk or Rock

Words and Music by Mark Ronson, Bruno Mars, Philip Lawrence, Jeff Bhasker, Devon Gallaspy, Nicholaus Williams, Lonnie Simmons, Ronnie Wilson, Charles Wilson, Rudolph Taylor and Robert Wilson

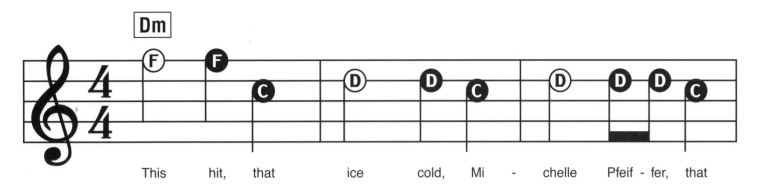

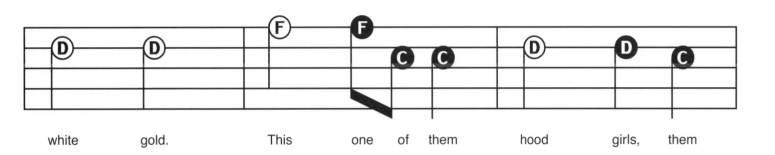

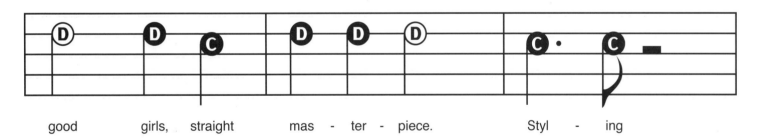

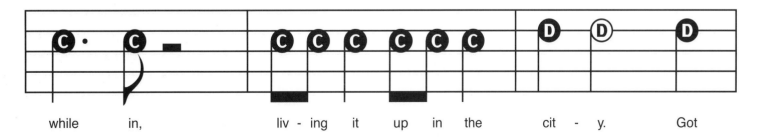

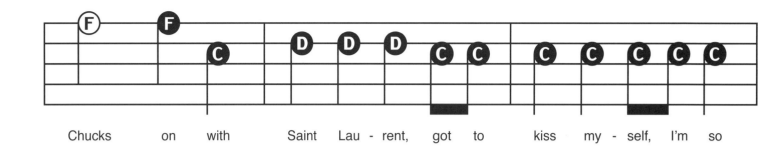

Chucks on with Saint Lau - rent, got to kiss my - self, I'm so

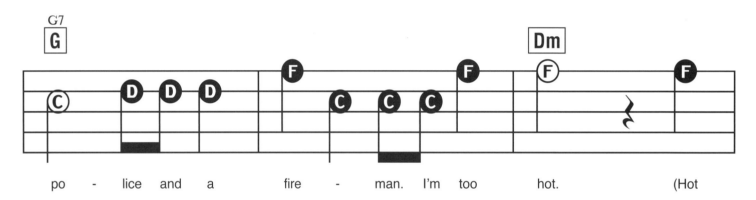

pret - ty. I'm too hot. (Hot damn.) Called the

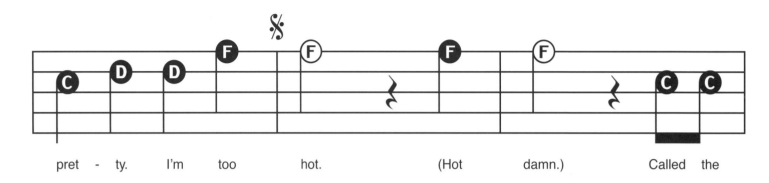

po - lice and a fire - man. I'm too hot. (Hot

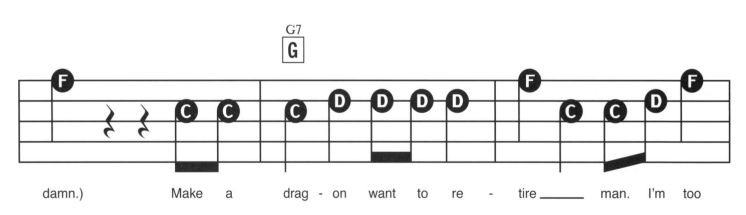

damn.) Make a drag - on want to re - tire _____ man. I'm too

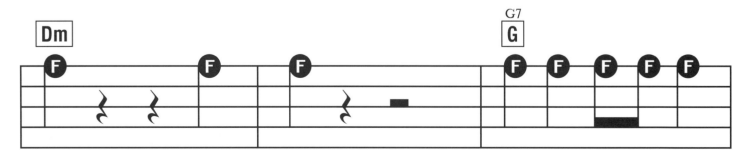

hot. (Hot damn.) Say my name, you know

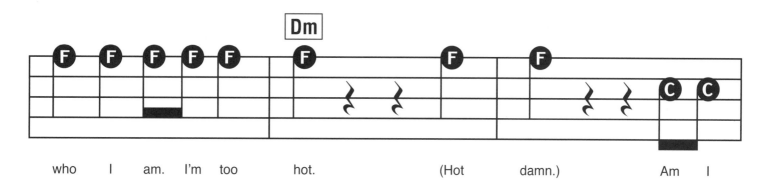

who   I   am.   I'm   too   hot.   (Hot   damn.)   Am   I

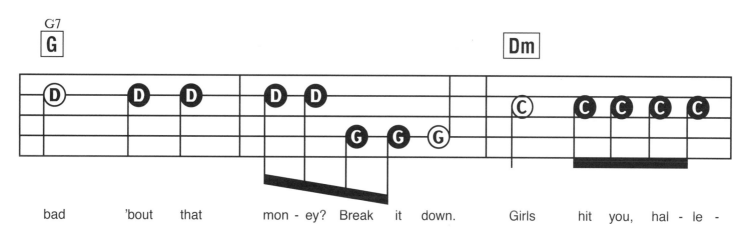

bad   'bout   that   mon - ey? Break   it   down.   Girls   hit   you, hal - le -

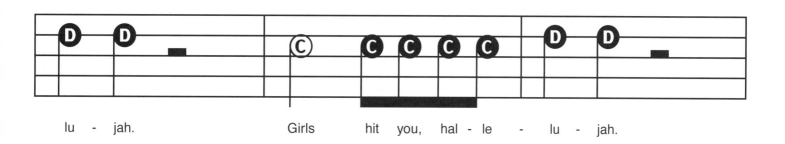

lu - jah.   Girls   hit   you, hal - le - lu - jah.

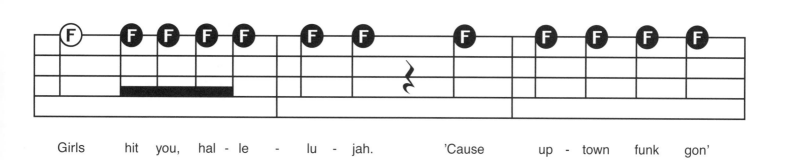

Girls   hit   you, hal - le - lu - jah.   'Cause   up - town funk gon'

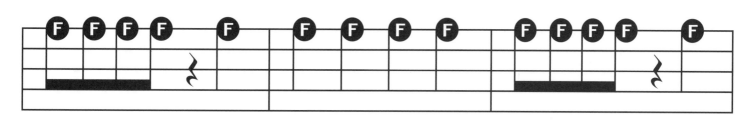

give   it   to you.   'Cause   up - town funk gon'   give   it   to you.   'Cause

76

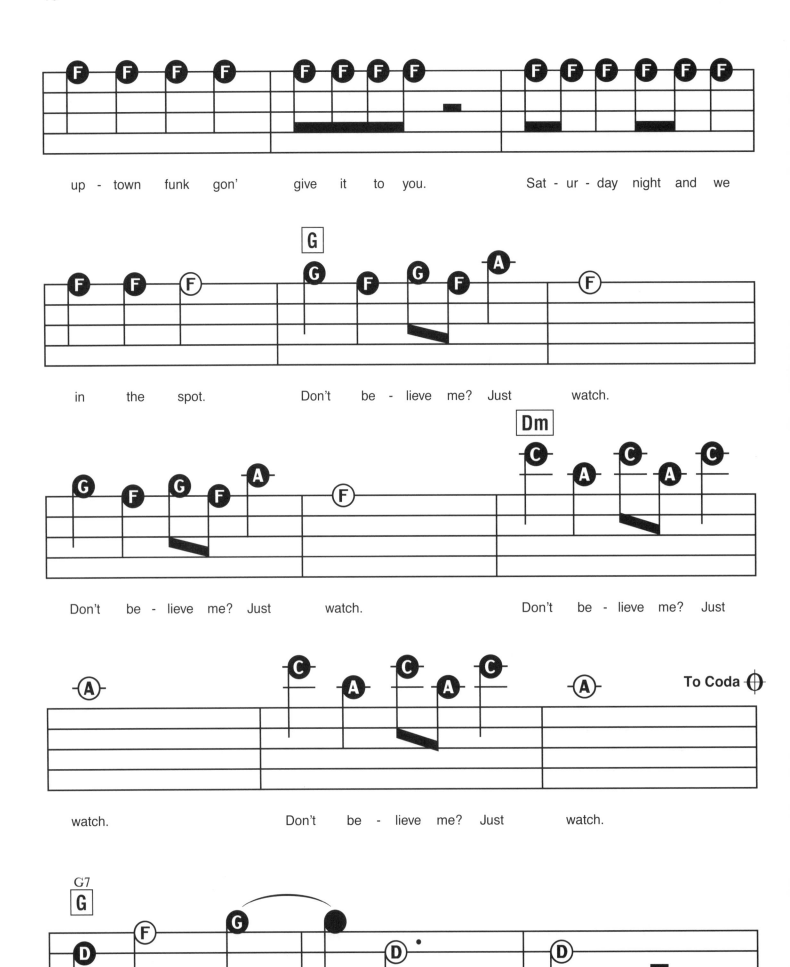

Dm

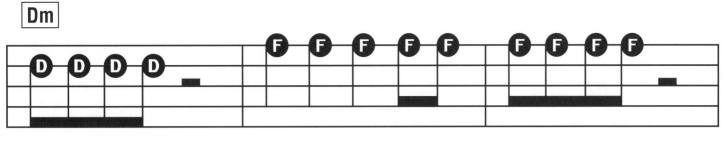

wait a min - ute, fill my cup, put some li - quor in it.

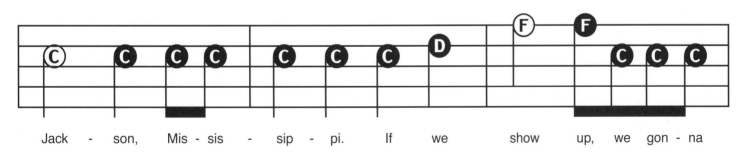

Take a sip, sign the check. Ju - li - o, get the

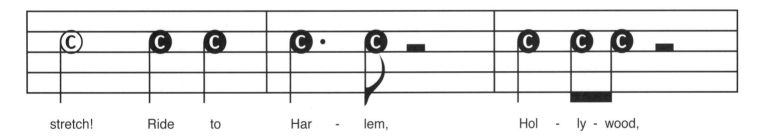

stretch! Ride to Har - lem, Hol - ly - wood,

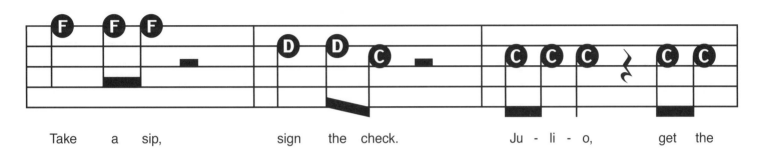

Jack - son, Mis - sis - sip - pi. If we show up, we gon - na

D.S. al Coda
(Return to 𝄋
Play to ⊕ and
Skip to Coda)

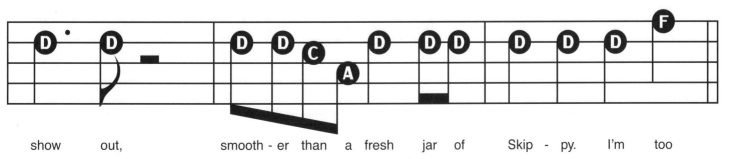

show out, smooth - er than a fresh jar of Skip - py. I'm too

78

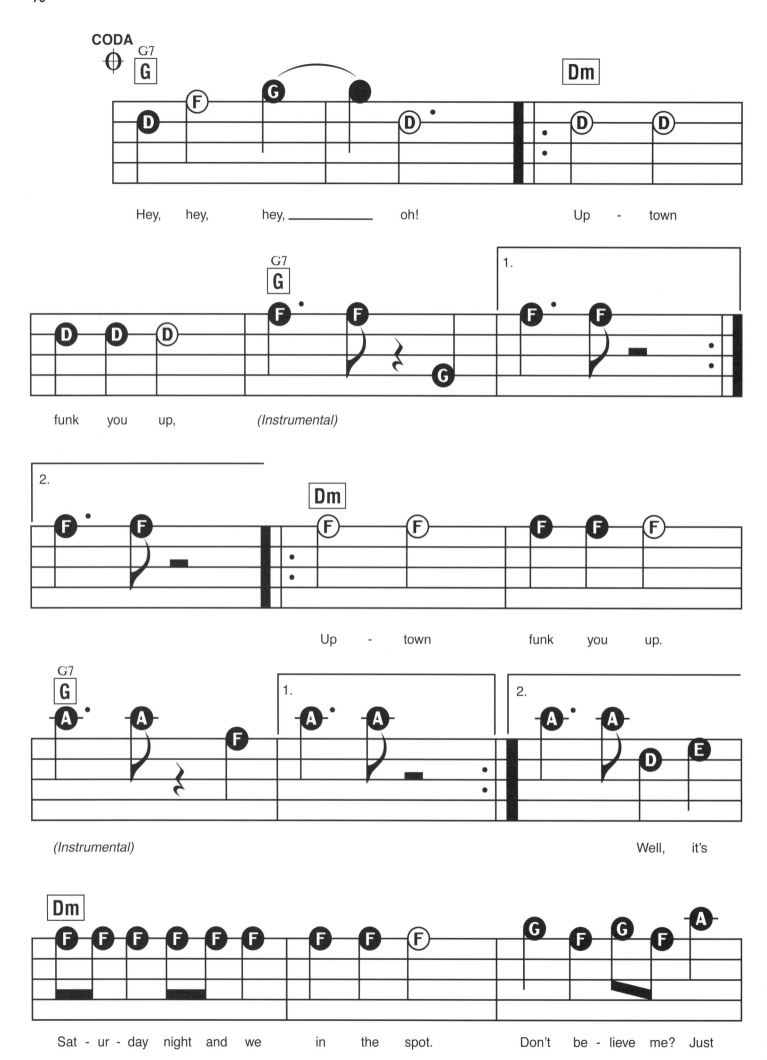

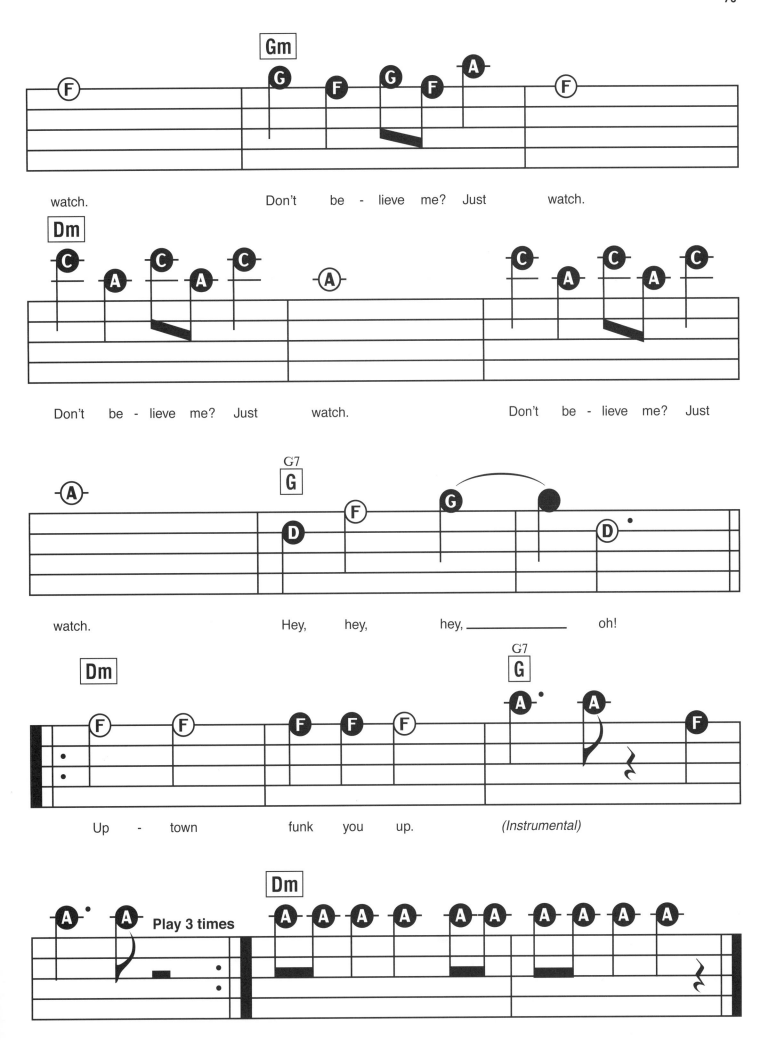

Registration Guide

• Match the Registration number on the song to the corresponding numbered category below. Select and activate an instrumental sound available on your instrument.

• Choose an automatic rhythm appropriate to the mood and style of the song. (Consult your Owner's Guide for proper operation of automatic rhythm features.)

• Adjust the tempo and volume controls to comfortable settings.

Registration

1	Mellow	Flutes, Clarinet, Oboe, Flugel Horn, Trombone, French Horn, Organ Flutes
2	Ensemble	Brass Section, Sax Section, Wind Ensemble, Full Organ, Theater Organ
3	Strings	Violin, Viola, Cello, Fiddle, String Ensemble, Pizzicato, Organ Strings
4	Guitars	Acoustic/Electric Guitars, Banjo, Mandolin, Dulcimer, Ukulele, Hawaiian Guitar
5	Mallets	Vibraphone, Marimba, Xylophone, Steel Drums, Bells, Celesta, Chimes
6	Liturgical	Pipe Organ, Hand Bells, Vocal Ensemble, Choir, Organ Flutes
7	Bright	Saxophones, Trumpet, Mute Trumpet, Synth Leads, Jazz/Gospel Organs
8	Piano	Piano, Electric Piano, Honky Tonk Piano, Harpsichord, Clavi
9	Novelty	Melodic Percussion, Wah Trumpet, Synth, Whistle, Kazoo, Perc. Organ
10	Bellows	Accordion, French Accordion, Mussette, Harmonica, Pump Organ, Bagpipes